EXPLORING
ANCIENT
CIVILIZATIONS

10

Stonehenge – Zoroastrianism

Marshall Cavendish

Sydney

Marshall Cavendish
99 White Plains Road
Tarrytown, New York 10591-9001

www.marshallcavendish.com

Consultants: Daud Ali, School of Oriental and African
Studies, University of London; Michael Brett, School
of Oriental and African Studies, London; John
Chinnery, School of Oriental and African Studies,
London; Philip de Souza; Joann Fletcher; Anthony
Green; Peter Groff, Department of Philosophy,
Bucknell University; Mark Handley, History
Department, University College London; Anders
Karlsson, School of Oriental and African Studies,
London; Alan Leslie, Glasgow University Archaeology
Research Department; Michael E. Smith, Department
of Anthropology, University at Albany; Matthew
Spriggs, Head of School of Archaeology and
Anthropology, Australian National University

Contributing authors: Richard Balkwill, Richard
Burrows, Peter Chrisp, Richard Dargie, Steve Eddy,
Clive Gifford, Jen Green, Peter Hicks, Robert Hull,
Jonathan Ingoldby, Pat Levy, Steven Maddocks, John
Malam, Saviour Pirotta, Stewart Ross, Sean Sheehan,
Jane Shuter

WHITE-THOMSON PUBLISHING
Editors: Alex Woolf and Steven Maddocks
Design: Derek Lee
Cartographer: Peter Bull Design
Picture Research: Glass Onion Pictures
Indexer: Fiona Barr

MARSHALL CAVENDISH
Editor: Thomas McCarthy
Editorial Director: Paul Bernabeo
Production Manager: Michael Esposito

Library of Congress Cataloging-in-Publication Data
Exploring ancient civilizations.
    p. cm.
Includes bibliographical references and indexes.
    ISBN 0-7614-7456-0 (set : alk. paper) -- ISBN 0-7614-7457-9 (v. 1 :
alk. paper) -- ISBN 0-7614-7458-7 (v. 2 : alk. paper) -- ISBN
0-7614-7459-5 (v. 3 : alk. paper) -- ISBN 0-7614-7460-9 (v. 4 : alk.
paper) -- ISBN 0-7614-7461-7 (v. 5 : alk. paper) -- ISBN 0-7614-7462-5
(v. 6 : alk. paper) -- ISBN 0-7614-7463-3 (v. 7 : alk. paper) -- ISBN
0-7614-7464-1 (v. 8 : alk. paper) -- ISBN 0-7614-7465-X (v. 9 : alk.
paper) -- ISBN 0-7614-7466-8 (v. 10 : alk. paper) -- ISBN 0-7614-7467-6
(v. 11 : alk. paper)
    1. Civilization, Ancient--Encyclopedias.
    CB311.E97 2004
    930'.03--dc21
                                                2003041224

ISBN 0-7614-7456-0 (set)
ISBN 0-7614-7466-8 (vol. 10)

Printed and bound in China

07 06 05 04 03 5 4 3 2 1

ILLUSTRATION CREDITS

AKG London: 724 (Justus Göpel), 730, 731, 733, 734 (François Guénet), 736, 739 (Erich
Lessing), 740 (Suzanne Held), 748 (John Hios), 749 (John Hios), 751 (Erich Lessing), 752
(Erich Lessing), 757 (Erich Lessing), 759 (Erich Lessing), 763, 766 (Henning Bock), 768
(Erich Lessing), 771 (Erich Lessing), 772 (Erich Lessing), 776 (Erich Lessing), 780 (Erich
Lessing), 781 (Erich Lessing), 782, (François Guénet), 793 (Erich Lessing).
Ancient Art and Architecture: 764, 767, 775 (Erich Lessing).
Art Archive: 745 (Dagli Orti).
Bridgeman Art Library: 725, 727 (British Museum, London), 728 (Ashmolean Museum,
Oxford), 729 (British Museum, London), 732 (Verulamium Museum, St. Alban's, UK), 735
(Lauros / Giraudon / Musée des Antiquités Nationales, St. Germain-en-Laye, France), 737
(Ali Meyer), 738, 743, 744 (Egyptian National Museum, Cairo), 747 (British Museum,
London), 750, 753 (Guildhall Library, London), 754, 755 (Hull and East Riding Museum,
Humberside, UK), 758 (Giraudon), 762 (Egyptian National Museum, Cairo), 765 (Phillips,
The International Fine Art Auctioneers), 769 (British Museum, London), 773 (Heini
Schneebeli), 774 (Peter Willi), 777 (National Museum of India, New Delhi), 778, 783
(Musée du Louvre, Paris), 784 (Egyptian National Museum, Cairo), 786 (Musée Rolin,
Autun, France), 787, 789 (Sean Sprague / Mexicolore), 791, 792 (Giraudon / National
Museum, Damascus, Syria), 794, 795 (Louvre, Paris), 796, 797, 798.
Corbis: 756.
Hutchison: 761.
N. J. Saunders: 790.
Topham: 760.
Werner Forman Archive: 741 (National Museum of Anthropology, Mexico City), 742, 746
(Museum für Völkerkunde, Basel, Switzerland), 779, 785.

Contents

Stonehenge

Stonehenge, the most important prehistoric monument in Britain, lies on Salisbury Plain in southern England. Stonehenge was built in three stages between 3020 and 2100 BCE; the famous standing stones were the final phase of its construction. The techniques used to raise these enormous stones are still largely a matter of conjecture.

The First Stonehenge

After the first stage of its construction (c. 3020–2900 BCE), Stonehenge was a circular soil bank and ditch enclosing an area 330 feet (100 m) in diameter. Within the enclosure stood a ring of fifty-six timber posts, forming a wooden circle 285 feet (86.7 m) in diameter. Two entrances passed through the bank and crossed the ditch. In stage two (c. 2900–2400 BCE), the timber circle was dismantled, parts of the ditch were filled in, and wooden posts were set up in the enclosure center.

Arrival of the Stones

During stage three (c. 2400–2100 BCE), the first stones arrived. Around eighty blocks of bluestone were brought to the site, each eight feet (2 m) tall and weighing 1.65 tons (1.5 t). The bluestone came from the Preseli Hills of southwestern Wales, far to the west. How it was brought to Stonehenge is the subject of debate. Some scholars believe it was quarried in Wales and transported over a distance of 240 miles (385 km); others argue the bluestones were carried to the area by a glacier and were left behind when it melted. What is known is that these stones were set upright in two horseshoe-shaped arcs in the middle of the enclosure. A pair of stones (one is called the Heel Stone) were positioned outside the main entrance, and four others were placed around the earth bank.

▼ Giant sarsens form the outer circle of Stonehenge, while smaller bluestones lie within it.

◀ From the air the full extent of the Stonehenge site can be seen, including the soil bank and ditch encircling the stone circle.

The bluestones were taken down around 2400 BCE, and a circle of local sarsen stone was erected. These massive stones, each weighing more than 27.5 tons (25,000 kg), came from the Marlborough Downs, twenty miles (30 km) to the north. Thirty sarsens were set in a circle, their tops capped with lintels (stones placed across the top of a pair of uprights) shaped to the curve of the ring. Five huge trilithons (two upright stones and a lintel) were placed inside the circle. Finally, the bluestones were reset within the sarsen circle.

How Was Stonehenge Built?

Stonehenge was built by the efforts of a well-organized workforce. The ditch and holes for timbers and stones were dug by hand using antler picks and shovels made from the shoulder blades of cattle. The stones were dragged to the site, possibly lashed to sledges that moved over wooden rollers. The surfaces of the sarsens were smoothed by pounding with stone balls, or maul stones. Each stone was then heaved upright, and its base was placed in a pit.

One estimate is that a team of 150 people per stone was needed for this task. Once the stones were upright, the lintels were put in place, probably inched up on a timber scaffold.

THE PURPOSE OF STONEHENGE

In the 1700s it was realized that the alignment of Stonehenge had astronomical significance. Since the 1960s the positions of its stones in relation to the sun and, to a lesser extent, the moon have been carefully studied. At daybreak on the first day of summer (June 21), the sun rises slightly west of the Heel Stone. Originally this stone had a partner, and the sun would have risen between them, bringing the first light of the longest day into the center of the circle. This fact suggests that Stonehenge was built as a sacred place connected with the worship of the sun.

SEE ALSO
- Avebury
- Prehistory

Sumer

Sumer is the name of the land in the southern part of the valley of Mesopotamia, between the Tigris and Euphrates Rivers, in present-day southern Iraq. Known as the cradle of civilization, Sumer was home to the world's first cities, and successive Sumerian civilizations made remarkable advances in language, politics, technology, and art.

The earliest widespread settlement of Sumer, between about 4500 and 4000 BCE, was by a people known as Ubaidians, who are so called after the name of the present-day village of Al-Ubaid, where evidence of their culture was first unearthed by archaeologists. The Ubaidians fished, farmed the rich soil, used stone tools, made pottery, and lived in small villages.

The Growth of Cities

The people known as Sumerians first emerged around 3500 BCE. The language they spoke (and later wrote in) eventually became the common language of the region.

The Sumerians lived together in small settlements and dug canals in the desert to irrigate the land to grow more food. By around 3000 BCE they began building the world's first towns and cities. Eridu was the first city, built over a Ubaidian settlement, and other cities, such as Ur and Erech, have also been found and excavated. In each city a central temple was constructed where the city's god was worshiped. Households were probably very alike, with little difference between them in terms of social class.

▼ The land of Sumer, where the world's first towns and cities emerged during the fourth and third millennia BCE

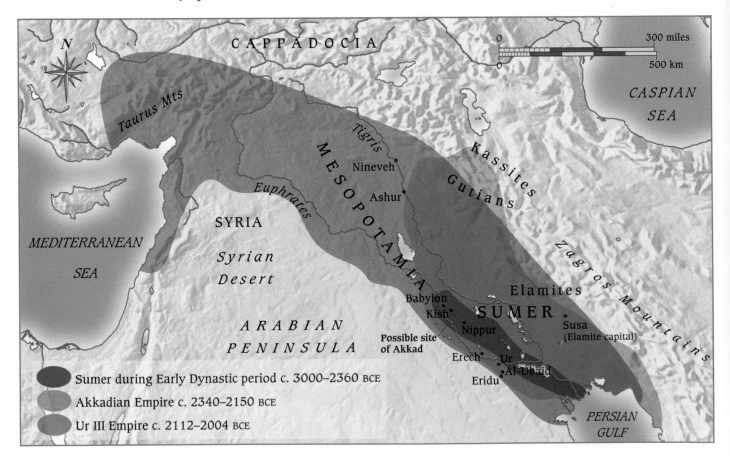

Sumer during Early Dynastic period c. 3000–2360 BCE

Akkadian Empire c. 2340–2150 BCE

Ur III Empire c. 2112–2004 BCE

SUMER

c. 4500–4000 BCE

Ubaidian culture flourishes in Sumer.

c. 3500 BCE

People known as the Sumerians emerge.

c. 3000 BCE

Cities such as Erech, Eridu, and Ur are established.

c. 2450 BCE

The Elamites conquer Sumer.

c. 2150 BCE

The Gutians conquer Sumer.

c. 2000 BCE

The Amorites conquer Sumer.

THE FOLLOWING LINES DESCRIBE THE CREATION OF THE WORLD'S FIRST CITY, ERIDU. THE SUMERIANS BELIEVED THAT THE FIRST LAND ROSE FROM THE SEA AT ERIDU AND THAT CIVILIZATION HAD ITS ORIGINS THERE. MARDUK, THE CHIEF BABYLONIAN GOD, IS DESCRIBED AS BUILDING A HOME FOR GODS AND HUMANS. THE ACCOUNT IS A REMINDER OF HOW THE FIRST CITIES HAD THEIR ORIGINS IN THE ALLUVIAL SOIL—THE "DIRT" OF THE POEM—FORMED BY THE SILT CARRIED DOWNSTREAM BY THE TIGRIS AND EUPHRATES RIVERS.

A brick had not been laid, a brick mold had not been built,
A house had not been made, a city had not been built . . .
All the lands were sea . . .
Marduk constructed a reed frame on the face of the waters.
He created dirt and poured it out by the reed frame.
In order to settle the gods in the dwelling of their hearts' delight,
He created mankind.

FROM AN ANCIENT MESOPOTAMIAN TEXT

The institution of kingship that gradually emerged in Sumer may have come about because conflict between towns or a need for protection from outside raiders led to the appointment of leaders. These leaders, perhaps with the help of priests, could have developed into kings by using religion to associate their families with the city's god.

▲ The impression made by this Sumerian cylinder seal, dating from around 2500 BCE, records a prayer to the god Marduk.

The Conquest of Sumer

As rivalry between different kings led to periods of internal conflict, other civilizations were able to take advantage of this division and conquer Sumer. The first people to do so were the Elamites, around 2450 BCE. Later, after the Akkadian king Sargon (reigned 2334–2284 BCE) conquered the cities of Sumer and brought them under one system of government, southern Mesopotamia became known as the "land of Sumer and Akkad."

This splendid jewelry, from a royal cemetery in the city of Ur, gives some indication of the high standard of Sumerian craft work.

Around 2150 BCE Akkadian rule came to an end, and Sumer was invaded by a nomadic people from the east called the Gutians. From around 2100 BCE there was a final flourish of Sumerian culture, associated with the Sumerian-speaking third-dynasty kings of the city of Ur, who apparently exercised an extreme form of state control.

The Amorites, another nomadic people, conquered all of Mesopotamia around 2000 BCE. The cities of Sumer were sacked, and temples were burned down and ransacked for their treasures. The people were killed, sold into slavery, or forced to abandon their way of life and move elsewhere. A Mesopotamian text describes the despair and sense of loss brought about by the invasions: "Ur is destroyed, bitter is its lament. . . . Our temple is destroyed, the gods have abandoned us, like migrating birds. Smoke lies on our city like a shroud."

Legacy

The culture of the Sumerians, which had contributed so much to the early history of civilization, continued to exert an influence on the cultures that supplanted it. The Babylonians worshiped many of the gods of Sumer, developed the Sumerian knowledge of the stars, made copies of Sumerian mythical stories, and lived in cities much like those of the people of Sumer.

The Cradle of Civilization

The land of Sumer is known as the cradle of civilization because it was there that a number of influential and far-reaching ideas and discoveries first emerged. Innovations such as writing, astronomy, wheeled vehicles, the potter's wheel, the idea of school, and the idea of mapping the world—all of which changed the face of civilization—developed for the first time in Sumer.

Perhaps the most remarkable development of all was the growth of urban life in cities. By 2000 BCE, nine out of ten Sumerians were living in cities. A major city, such as Uruk, could have had as many as 36,000 adult males living in it.

Arts and Crafts

Most of what is known about the achievements of Sumer—from written texts as well as from artifacts—is the result of archaeological work. As well as the remains of large temples, a rich variety of artifacts has been unearthed, from everyday objects, such as pottery, to precious jewelry and musical instruments. The Sumerians were talented craftspeople. Bowls crafted from alabaster were polished with sand to make them smooth to the touch.

▼ *This game board, another find from the royal cemetery in the city of Ur, suggests that Sumerian royalty enjoyed their leisure time.*

LAW CODES

Hundreds of thousands of clay tablets from Mesopotamia have been unearthed, including some that are copies of a set of legal rules, a law code, first written down in the city of Ur in Sumer. One of the earliest-known examples of a law code, it is associated with the king Ur-Nammu or possibly his better-known son Shulgi. The law code is a list of laws covering situations such as adultery, divorce, escaped slaves, witchcraft, and disputes over the ownership of land. The code of Ur-Nammu dates from around 2100 BCE. Another law code has also been discovered that refers to a period about 150 years later and deals with cases involving marriages and contracts arising from the sale and ownership of land.

Game boards were inlaid with patterns of colored shells, and items of personal jewelry were adorned with miniature designs such as leaves and pomegranates. Delicate musical instruments, especially stringed instruments, such as harps, were adorned with the heads of bulls in gold.

Literature

One of the most enduring legacies of Sumer is its literature, especially its myths, which were written down on clay tablets and copied by scribes for many centuries after the decline of Sumerian civilization. Among the best known are the Gilgamesh stories, posssibly based on the exploits of a king of Sumer who lived around 2700 BCE.

ENHEDUANNA

Enheduanna, a daughter of King Sargon, was a priestess of the moon god in Ur. She lived around the beginning of the twenty-third century BCE and was credited by the Babylonians as the editor of hymns for a temple at Eridu and as an author in her own right—thus, she is the world's first known female author. The hymns she edited were copied by scribes long after her death, and some have survived on clay tablets. Her own writing has also survived in a tale about the goddess Ishtar that also concerns Enheduanna's own role as priestess. Ur and other Sumerian cities rebelled against Akkadian rule, and Enheduanna's position as priestess was challenged. The success of Ishtar in Enheduanna's tale may well reflect her own success in holding on to her position.

◀ *Found in a king's tomb in Ur, this bull's head decorates a musical stringed instrument from around 2500 BCE.*

SEE ALSO
- Akkadians • Babylonians • Elamites
- Erech • Eridu • Gilgamesh Epic • Ishtar
- Mesopotamia • Sargon of Akkad
- Shulgi • Ur

Tacitus

Most scholars agree that Publius Cornelius Tacitus (c. 56–c. 120 CE) was the greatest of Roman historians. He wrote several books about Roman history and about the lives of Rome's first emperors. For modern historians Tacitus is a vital source of information on the Roman world of the first century CE.

The Life of Tacitus

Little is known about Tacitus's early life. It is thought that his family lived either in southern France, perhaps at Vasio (present-day Vaison-la-Romaine) or in northern Italy. Not even his praenomen (first name) is known with certainty; although most scholars believe it was Publius, some think it could have been Gaius. By around 75 CE, Tacitus was in Rome, where, as a teenager, he studied oratory, the art of public speaking. Oratory was a higher-education subject taught by a specialist teacher known as a rhetor. Only boys studied oratory, as it was believed to be unnecessary for girls. Students came from high-ranking families, and once they had mastered the rules of speech making, they looked forward to careers in politics and the law.

Tacitus set his sights on becoming a politician. In 77 or 78 CE he married the daughter of Gnaeus Julius Agricola (40–93 CE), the Roman military governor of Britain. Around the same time Emperor Vespasian (reigned 69–79 CE) granted him permission to wear a toga decorated with a wide purple stripe along its edge. "Wearing the purple" was a sign that Tacitus was allowed to stand for the position of senator in the Roman government, which he attained. In 97 he became a consul, a job that was held for one year at a time.

▶ Tacitus is widely regarded as an accurate commentator on the Roman world.

► These writing materials used by the Romans include a pottery inkwell and, below it, a replica of a wooden writing tablet. The tablet would have been covered with a thin layer of wax, and text would have been scratched into it with a pointed pen called a stylus.

As a consul Tacitus would have passed sentence on criminals and presided over games and festivals held in Rome. He gave the funeral address for a fellow consul, Lucius Verginius Rufus, at which, no doubt, he used all of his public-speaking skills. In 112 or 113 Tacitus was appointed governor of the Roman province of Asia, another government position typically held for a year. Tacitus died a few years later, around 120.

Writer and Historian

Among Tacitus's most celebrated works is the *Life of Julius Agricola*, his first work, which was published in 98. This biography of his father-in-law contains valuable information about Britain as a province of the Roman Empire. Other works include the *Origin of the Germans*, a history of the German people, and two histories of the Roman people, the *Histories* and the *Annals*. Modern historians regard Tacitus as a reliable and trustworthy author who took great care to ensure his facts were accurate and whose writing sheds much light on the Roman world of two thousand years ago.

TACITUS DESCRIBES THE PERSECUTION OF THE CHRISTIANS BY NERO.

Nero . . . punished with the utmost refinements of cruelty, a class of men, loathed for their vices, whom the crowd styled Christians . . . vast numbers were convicted, not so much on the count of arson, as for hatred of the human race. And derision accompanied their end: they were covered with wild beasts' skins and torn to death by dogs; or they were fastened on crosses, and when daylight failed were burned to serve as lamps by night.

TACITUS, ANNALS, 15:44

SEE ALSO

• Roman Republic and Empire

Technology

The word *technology* comes from the ancient Greek *techne*, meaning "making," or "crafting." Technology generally involves fashioning some device, machine, or tool with which to alter some part of the natural world. Technological development began in prehistoric times with simple tools such as sticks, used to break up soil, and pieces of sharp-edged stone, used to scrape animal hides. Over thousands of years, technology grew in complexity as people sought to influence and control the world around them.

Simple Machines

It is generally agreed by engineers that there are five basic pieces of technology. Those five objects are the inclined plane (or, in its smaller form, the wedge), the lever, the wheel, the screw, and the pulley. Humans throughout history have based a whole range of machines on these five simple devices, either individually or in some combination.

All five simple machines were used in ancient times. The lever and the wedge originated in prehistoric times, when people used tree branches as levers to move rocks and wedge-shaped stones to split logs. The inclined plane and the pulley, both of which are essential for raising heavy loads, were in use over 4,500 years ago, when the Egyptians started to build pyramids.

The first examples of wheels were found in Mesopotamia and date from some time between 3000 and 3500 BCE. An early use of the screw was in screw presses. These machines squeezed all the juice out of fruits to make wine and other drinks. By the beginning of the first century CE, the Romans were using screw presses to produce olive oil.

◀ *The manufacturing stages of a hatchet from the New Stone Age, with raw stone on the left and the finished tool on the right.*

Irrigation Technology

An essential factor in the early development of agriculture was the creation of a technology that could bring water to fields in large quantities. Some civilizations, such as the Chavín in South America, diverted entire rivers and channeled water to their fields along stone canals. Others, such as the Sumerians, built dams across rivers to create reservoirs of water. Aqueducts were constructed to carry this water long distances from the reservoirs to fields. The Egyptians were using irrigation canals to channel Nile floodwater as early as 3100 BCE. One particularly important piece of technology was the shadoof, a long lever with a weight at one end and a bucket to lift water at the other. Peoples in both ancient India and Egypt were using the shadoof as early as 1400 BCE.

Iron making

Historians believe that iron making began in the Hittite Empire during the second millennium BCE. After the downfall of the Hittites in 1200 BCE, knowledge of how to smelt metal from iron ore spread rapidly throughout Europe and western Asia. The development of iron enabled new and tougher tools to be created, particularly tools with sharp cutting edges, such as the plow, the spade, and the ax. Iron making also greatly influenced early agriculture, as stronger iron tools were better able to break up heavy soils and make them suitable for cultivating crops. The ancient Chinese had learned how to produce iron by 600 BCE, and about a century later, they learned how to make cast iron by adding carbon to the metal while it was still in its molten form.

Power Technology

In all ancient civilizations, humans and animals provided the energy that powered machines and technology. Many ancient civilizations developed methods of maximizing the energy from these sources, such as more efficient harnesses for horses and oxen and wheels that traveled more smoothly.

WATERWHEELS AND WATER MILLS

Only one practical alternative to human and animal power was developed in the ancient world: waterpower. Around the first century CE waterwheels were developed to harness the natural power of water as it fell from a height or traveled downstream in a river. Remains of waterwheels dating from around this time have been found in China, India, and areas of Europe that were then part of the Roman Empire.

A waterwheel consists of a set of paddles mounted around a wheel. The force of the water moves the paddles and thus causes the wheel to turn. In Syria by 100 CE, the turning wheel was fitted with a series of tubes or buckets to create an irrigation waterwheel: the buckets filled with water when at the bottom and emptied their load into a chute or channel when at the top. This water could then flow along channels and irrrigate farmland.

The turning axle (the shaft at the center of the waterwheel) could also be used to power other machines. The most common use of the waterwheel in ancient times was as the power generator of a water mill. The waterwheel's axle, driving a heavy millstone or pounding hammer, crushed different types of cereal and grain to make flour. The largest known ancient water mill complex was found in southern France. Built around 300 CE by the Romans, it consisted of two banks of eight waterwheels supplied with water from a Roman aqueduct. This water mill could probably grind twenty-seven tons of grain every day.

▲ The remains of a Roman well, used to draw water up from deep underground reserves, in Tuna-el-Gebel, Egypt.

► *Hero of Alexandria demonstrates his steam-driven aeolipile to other Alexandrian scholars.*

HERO OF ALEXANDRIA

Hero (or Heron) lived sometime between the second century BCE and the first century CE in Alexandria, Egypt. A mathematician and scientist, Hero experimented with and wrote about hydraulics and pneumatics but is best known as an ingenious inventor, especially of the aeolipile, or "windball."

Like many of the engines and turbines of the modern world, the aeolipile used steam as a form of power. The steam from a sealed cauldron of boiling water was sent via two pipes into a metal ball. As the steam was expelled from the ball through two curved exhaust pipes, the ball was sent spinning around at high speed.

The aeolipile was just one of eighty different machines Hero is believed to have invented, including fountains powered by air pressure, a primitive surveying device called a *dioptra*, and the first coin-operated slot machine. Used in temples, this machine dispensed a small portion of water for cleaning hands when a coin of a certain weight was deposited.

The ancient Greeks developed a compound pulley, a machine in which a number of pulleys were all used in combination. Compound pulleys helped to amplify (increase) the force exerted so that, with the same effort, more weight could be lifted.

Wind power was harnessed to a more limited extent in ancient times—sails were used to drive boats and ships. The harnessing of wind power to drive a machine did not occur until about the seventh century CE. The first known examples of windmills are found in what is now Iraq and date from around 650 CE.

SEE ALSO
- Aqueducts • Cities • Houses and Homes
- Hygiene and Sanitation • Roads • Science
- Transportation • Warfare and Conquest
- Weights and Measures

Temples

Temples are places of worship; in ancient times they were often believed to house the spirit of the god or gods to whom they were dedicated. In ancient temples priests performed rituals and, in some civilizations, offered sacrifices. Larger temple complexes provided homes for priests and religious communities. A temple was often the most important building in a city. As such, many temples represent their culture's finest architectural achievements.

The First Temples

Some prehistoric peoples believed that their gods lived among trees. The earliest temples were sacred groves. The early Greeks believed that the rustling of tree branches was in fact the voices of the gods foretelling the future.

By the fourth millennium BCE, Neolithic people were carving simple cave-like temples out of rocks. Remains have been found as far afield as India, Egypt, China, and the Mediterranean island of Malta.

Other temples on Malta were built above ground from massive slabs of stone. The most famous example is Hagar Qim, built between 3600 and 3500 BCE. Its mushroom-shaped altars, on which animals were sacrificed, still survive. Archaeologists have also found carvings representing the tree of life and statues of a mother goddess, but little is known about the people who worshiped there.

Mesopotamian Temples

Early sacred sites were often situated on high ground in the belief that worshipers might thereby be as close to the gods as possible. The territory of the Assyrians and Babylonians was largely flat, however, so they built stepped pyramids, up to three hundred feet (91 m) high, and placed their temples at the top. There were benches on the steps, where the faithful could rest on their way up. Kings and priests performed ceremonies in these shrines, while the common people prayed below.

▼ On the Mediterranean island of Malta is the world's oldest known human structure—the Neolithic temple of Hagar Qim, whose carvings, altars, and chambers were constructed using nothing more than flint and obsidian tools.

▶ *The Buddhist rock-cut cave temples in Ajanta, western India, date from the first century* BCE *and contain fresco paintings that depict colorful Buddhist myths and legends.*

Egyptian Temples

The Egyptians considered the Nile River the source of life, and so they built many of their temples along its banks. The temple at Karnak, for example, was an enormous complex. More than 81,000 Egyptians were employed to work in the temple and on the surrounding land. They worked in the fields, workshops, food stores, and library.

Most Egyptian temple complexes were surrounded by a high wall. Inside there was a man-made lake, where the priests conducted purifying ceremonies. The inner part of most temples contained at least one court, which was reached through an immense doorway flanked by towers, or pylons. The court itself had no roof and was surrounded by colonnaded passages.

Beyond the court of many larger temples was a vast chamber, known as the hypostyle hall. The other chambers within were open only to the high priests and the pharaoh himself. There, in daily rituals, the priests looked after the statues of the gods, treating them with utmost reverence as they washed them and dressed them in fine linen. During festivals, large numbers of people assembled outside the temples to watch the statues of the gods paraded around the grounds or set afloat in the man-made lake on sacred boats.

Greek Temples

Around 1000 BCE, Greek temples were made mostly of wood and sun-dried bricks. By the sixth century BCE, the Greeks were building magnificent temples of marble and polished stone. The Greeks saw their temples mainly as houses of the gods rather than places for worshipers to gather.

Greek temples were usually built in high places. Inside was a large statue of the god to whom the temple was dedicated. Every morning, the sunlight fell on the statue through the temple doorway, which always faced east. The roofs of big temples were supported by two rows of columns. They divided the space into a central hall (a nave) and two aisles. Treasure was often kept in the temple, as it was the safest place in the town or city.

Indian Temples

Whereas the ancient Greeks and Romans built their temples on hills and in wide, open spaces, Indian Buddhists preferred to carve their temples out of rock. Massive caves with ornate facades were carved in stone near present-day Mumbai (Bombay) from around 255 BCE to 300 CE. These temples were places of worship and were visited by pilgrims, many of whom had traveled great distances to seek the holy men's wisdom.

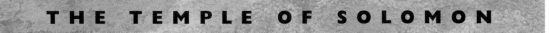

THE TEMPLE OF SOLOMON

Originally built in the tenth century BCE, the Temple of Solomon in Jerusalem was made of stone, timber, and metal. Based on Phoenician design, it had a large rectangular hall, the naos, that led into the holy of holies, a chamber where the ark of the covenant, the sacred chest that held the Ten Commandments, was kept. Only priests were allowed in this part of the temple. It was believed that a common person who touched the ark would die in the greatest agony.

The temple was destroyed in 587 BCE and rebuilt between 20 and 18 BCE. In 70 CE this second temple, too, was razed to the ground when the Romans destroyed Jerusalem. The remaining wall, called the Western (or Wailing) Wall, is the most sacred Jewish site in the world.

◀ A model of the Temple of Solomon in Jerusalem as it would have looked during the time of Herod the Great, king of Judaea from 37 to 4 BCE.

▲ *These elaborate carvings adorn the entrance to a Buddhist cave temple in Shanxi Province, China, that was built between 460 and 494 CE.*

Roman Temples

Many temples in ancient Rome were vast and square, although others were circular or in the shape of polygons. The central part of the temple was called a *cella*. Inside the *cella* was the statue of the god to whom the temple was dedicated. Roman temples were built in such a way that the rising sun would shine on the statue on the god's birthday.

On the steps outside the temple was a huge altar where priests made sacrifices to the gods. Unlike their Greek counterparts, however, Roman priests did not spend their entire life in the service of the temple but carried out other important work in the community.

IN EGYPTIAN TEMPLES SOME PRIESTESSES DANCED WHILE OTHERS CHANTED VERSES SUCH AS THESE:

Exalted is Hathor, she of love!

. . . .

She is exalted on this free day!
On this free day, O Sonebi . . .

Christian Temples

The early Christians, who were sometimes persecuted by the Roman authorities for refusing to worship the ancient gods, used catacombs as their first temples. Catacombs were tomb complexes cut out of rock, just as were the first temples of ancient history. After Emperor Constantine made the practice of Christianity legal in the Roman Empire in 313 CE, Christians began to use huge temples to accommodate the large number of people who had started to worship Jesus Christ. These temples were not like those that had been the homes of the ancient gods. Rather, they resembled huge indoor markets with a central hall, called a nave, a corridor on either side, and an apse (chamber) at one end. To this day, many Christian churches are laid out in the same way.

Teotihuacán

Teotihuacán started around 1000 BCE as a small village in the Valley of Mexico and grew into one of the greatest Mesoamerican cities. Much of the great settlement has been restored, including the massive Pyramid of the Sun, which is over 200 feet (61 m) high. The restored city lies thirty-one miles (50 km) from Mexico City.

Teotihuacán was planned carefully in the form of a grid. The center of this grid is the three-mile (5 km) Street of the Dead. Its name is translated from the Aztec word *miccaotli*, and historians think it refers to the tombs and shrines that once bordered the wide avenue.

Alongside this central avenue were a remarkable number of buildings, including pyramids, a huge marketplace, a plaza with workshops, and several residential areas. In 50 BCE over 40,000 people lived in Teotihuacán. By 500 CE this figure had grown to an astonishing 150,000—many times more than lived in any European city at the time. Some inhabitants came and settled from other parts of Mesoamerica, such as Oaxaca in present-day Mexico.

Teotihuacán, itself sited on a plateau, was surrounded by mountains that were a good source of obsidian, a volcanic glass used to make knife blades, carved ornaments, and mirrors. The highland climate was arid, and natural springs within the city provided a vital water supply. Canals and irrigation channels were built to carry the water to cultivated fields outside the city.

Art and Craft

Carvings and painted murals once filled the buildings of Teotihuacán. Common images and themes included life's two most basic necessities: maize and water. The jaguar appears in many forms—part real, part fantastic—and is usually linked with bird and serpent images.

◀ This reconstructed mural from Teotihuacán shows a priest in a richly decorated cloak. His face is covered by a feathered mask.

Historians believe the location of the Pyramid of the Sun is of particular significance. Underneath this massive pyramid is a cave with separate chambers where, in 1970, archaeologists discovered offerings to gods. The pyramid may have been thought of as a link to the spirit world beneath the earth.

The pyramid, with five sets of steps to the top, allowed the people of Teotihuacán to observe the movements of the sun and stars and to perform religious rituals honoring the subterranean spirit world—the source of life and the place to which people were believed to return after death.

▲ The Pyramid of the Sun towers two hundred feet (61 m) above the Street of the Dead. In the foreground of the picture are the smaller pyramids of the ciudadela (city area).

The towers of Teotihuacán were dominated by images of the feathered serpent Quetzalcoatl and the fire serpent, which was depicted carrying the sun on its daily journey across the sky. Other images survive of the storm god in the Palace of Tepantlitla, an imaginary paradise filled with birds, butterflies, and flowers and an abundant supply of water.

Decline

It seems that as Teotihuacán grew larger, the city came under increasing attack by invaders and rivals. Around 650 CE, Teotihuacán was sacked and burned, and many buildings at the center of the city were destroyed.

The landscape around Teotihuacán may have been eroded by destruction of the forests for firewood. This erosion could have led to fields wearing out or disappearing. Some evidence suggests that Teotihuacán suffered serious droughts.

After 500 CE, Teotihuacán began to lose its status as a unified city state, and many of its citizens drifted back to their homelands in the surrounding country. By 800 CE the influence of the great city was at an end.

Thebes

Thebes was a city in ancient Egypt situated on the east bank of the Nile River. Its Egyptian name was Waset ("city of the scepter"); it was later called Thebes by the Greeks. The modern city of Luxor now stands on the site of Thebes. On the opposite bank of the Nile is the Valley of the Kings.

A Center of Power

During the Old Kingdom, which lasted from 2686 to 2181 BCE, Thebes was a small town. From 2181 to 2055 BCE, Egypt was divided into Upper and Lower Egypt. Upper Egypt was ruled from Thebes, and eventually the Theban rulers took over all of Egypt and ruled it as one kingdom. As the Eleventh Dynasty, they ruled until around 1985 BCE. The first king of the Twelfth Dynasty, Amenemhat I, moved the capital north to Itjtawy, which was south of Memphis.

During the second intermediate period (1640–1550 BCE), most of Egypt was ruled by the Hyksos people from the Levant. In 1550 BCE, the Thebans again took control of Egypt. Although the administrative capital remained at Memphis, in the Nile Delta region, Thebes held its status as Egypt's most important city and religious capital.

A Religious Center

When Thebes became the principal city of Egypt in 2050 BCE, it grew in importance as a religious center. Ancient Egypt had many gods and goddesses. Certain gods sometimes rose in importance because they were the local gods of the ruling pharaoh. The local god of Thebes, Amun, came to be worshiped throughout Egypt, and the largest and most important temple to Amun was built near Thebes at Karnak.

◀ The Temple of Amun at Luxor was begun in about 1360 BCE by the pharaoh Amenhotep III and enlarged by later pharaohs. Each year a statue of Amun was carried to this temple from the Temple of Amun at Karnak.

The legend of Thebes exceeds any city.
In the beginning hers were the waters and the dry land;
The sands came to mark off fields and form the high hill she stands on.
And then men set up the city, each with his own calling;
Setting up Thebes, God's eye over Egypt.
Each city stirs into life from the breath of an invisible god.
Each burns to be great
Like Thebes: hers is the light of perfection.

A Burial Center

By 1550 BCE the desert on the west bank of the river, opposite Thebes, had become an important burial place, later known as the Valley of the Kings. Queens and other members of the royal family were buried nearby in the Valley of the Queens, and nobles were buried near the Valley of the Kings, at Qurna. This necropolis, or city of the dead, became so important that the west bank of Thebes had its own mayor and officials to administer it. Even when much of the power was moved away from Thebes after 1295 BCE, the pharaohs and their families continued to be buried in the Valley of the Kings and the Valley of the Queens. The last royal burials took place there around 1069 BCE.

Decline

From about 1069 BCE, Thebes began to decline in importance. By around 700 BCE, Egypt had been ruled from cities in the north for so long that many people had forgotten that Thebes had once been so powerful. When the Greeks took over Egypt in the fourth century BCE, it became part of an empire focused on the Mediterranean, and the coastal city of Alexandria became the capital.

◀ *This jewel, in the shape of a scarab beetle, was found in the tomb of the pharaoh Tutankhamen, who was buried in the Valley of the Kings in 1327 BCE.*

SEE ALSO
• Amun • Egypt • Egyptian Mythology
• Tutankhamen • Valley of the Kings

Tikal

Tikal, one of the great city-states of the Mayan civilization, flourished between 150 BCE and 800 CE. Substantial ruins remain in the northern part of Guatemala in Central America. Situated deep within the rain forest, some of the largest buildings have been well preserved over the years in the thick vegetation.

Growth and Decline

In about 600 BCE Tikal was a small community that traded in obsidian, a volcanic glass used to make ornaments and tools. Around 150 BCE, the city grew in size very quickly, and large ceremonial buildings were constructed.

The city was rebuilt and further expanded from about 200 CE by its ambitious rulers. Rivalry with other cities arose, especially with nearby Uaxactun. A long war, culminating in a big battle in 378, saw the capture of Uaxactun by a general known as Smoking Frog.

Like other centers of the Mayan civilization, Tikal declined and decayed from about 800. Historians think that of the reasons offered for the decline, the most likely is that growing crops for so many people in one place exhausted the land.

Buildings

Some of the biggest structures at Tikal were built in the northern acropolis, the religious and cultural center of Tikal. These included tall pyramids—monuments to the dead, who were sometimes buried underneath them. The Maya saw close connections between the living and the dead and also between the lords who ruled over the people and the gods whom they worshiped.

Another major structure in Tikal was the central acropolis, a palace built on a platform with only a few entrances and decorated with many carvings and delicate colored designs.

◀ A view of the northern acropolis at Tikal, surrounded by dense vegetation. The tallest pyramids are monuments to the dead.

THE TEMPLE OF THE JAGUAR

The tallest pyramid at Tikal was nearly 200 feet high. At the top was a famous temple, known as the Temple of the Jaguar, where the kings and high priests conducted ceremonies and performed rituals, including bloodletting and human sacrifice. They thought these acts would bring them into closer contact with their gods.

To the Maya, the jaguar was a symbol of strength, power, and mystery. People believed that when darkness fell each day, the jaguar looked after the sun on its journey through the night. They saw its shape in the stars, and many of the paintings and carvings at Tikal included images of jaguars, often in combination with the outlines of snakes and birds.

▲ This carving, part of a lintel (a wooden beam over a doorway) in Temple IV at Tikal, shows a Mayan lord, with panels of glyphs on either side.

On the highest floor of the central acropolis is the throne room, where the *ahau*, the king and high priest of Tikal, would decide on acts of war, receive visitors from other cities, and administer justice. Around the acropolis, stelae (engraved stone monuments) record historical events and commemorate the achievements of great leaders.

Life in the City

Families lived together in big houses in large communities outside the city center. They shared responsibility for growing food, cultivating the ground, and ensuring a water supply was available for the large number of inhabitants to survive.

Great rulers were buried in royal tombs. Sometimes a portrait head or a face mask would be attached to the body. Some of these masks, which were made of fuchsite (a hard stone) and carved with a crown and headdress, have survived.

SEE ALSO
• Maya • Pyramids

Tombs

Tombs are constructed to house the bodies of the dead and to act as a focus for honoring the dead and for remembering their lives. The oldest surviving tombs in the world are in Beijing, China, and date back at least 400,000 years. Fundamental to most ancient religions was a belief in the afterlife, and many civilizations buried their dead with possessions and sometimes family members, servants, and animals that were thought to be of use to the dead in the afterlife. As such, excavated tombs provide archaeologists and historians with a rich source of information about life in the ancient world.

The Graves of Ur

In the Sumerian city of Ur, which flourished around 2400 BCE, people were buried in underground chambers cut into sloping ground. The bodies were laid on their side with their hands clasped at the chest. Possessions (including jewelry, cylinder seals, and bowls) were laid out around the bodies.

The royal families of Ur, along with their slaves, grooms, soldiers, and attendants, were buried in domed chambers set at the bottom of deep pits. The sides and floors of the pits were covered in reed matting. A ramp led down to a door in the pit, which was sealed shut after the funeral. Tomb guards—the bodies of men who had taken poison to join their ruler in the afterlife—were buried at the door in the belief that they would stop anyone from entering.

Leonard Woolley, a British archaeologist who carried out excavations at Ur, discovered the grave of Queen Pu-abi in 1926. He believed that chapels once stood above the royal burial chambers. The lavishness of these tombs indicate that the high-ranking people of Ur believed their power would continue into the afterlife.

▼ Archaeologists uncovered one of the richest hoards of treasure ever found when they excavated the royal cemetery at Ur in the 1920s. Among the finds was this royal standard of Ur, which had a peace side (shown below) and a war side.

Egyptian Pyramids and Tombs

The first Egyptian pyramid was built around 2650 BCE as a burial place for King Djoser. It was designed with stepped sides by his special architect Imhotep. In the reign of King Sneferu (reigned c. 2613–2589 BCE), the first pyramid with smooth sides was constructed, the shape symbolizing the mound of earth that rose out of the primeval waters at the beginning of time. King Khufu's Great Pyramid, the largest ever built, was completed around 2566 BCE. Inside it, narrow passages led to the king's burial chamber, where the king's body lay surrounded by magnificent treasures.

The pyramids were often broken into by grave robbers, so from around 1504 BCE the Egyptian pharaohs were buried in underground tombs in the Valley of the Kings near Thebes. These tombs also had magnificent burial chambers, known as the halls of gold, which were cut into the cliffs, many of them high up to make them inaccessible to robbers. Despite this precaution, almost all the tombs were robbed in ancient times.

Greek Cremation

The ancient Greeks of the Mycenaean period, which lasted from around 1650 to 1200 BCE, buried their dead in underground tombs. Above each tomb was an altar with a funnel leading through the ground; the funnel allowed liquid offerings to be poured to the dead below.

The Greeks of the later classical period cremated the bodies of the dead so that ghosts would not be able to haunt their relatives. The ashes were placed in special jars called amphorae and buried outside the city. Grave markers, made from wood, stone, or pottery, were often in the shape of jars. Sometimes stone pillars were erected, decorated with inscriptions and carvings and frequently showing mythological creatures, such as sirens. Food offerings were left at the graves to sustain the dead on their way to the next world.

▶ *The Mycenaean graves of the fourteenth and thirteenth centuries BCE are arranged in circles and consist of a long rectangular shaft that leads down to a stone-walled burial chamber. For this reason, they are sometimes known as shaft graves.*

It was very important for Greek people to be buried in their homeland. When a person died away from home, relatives often built a special grave, called a cenotaph, in which a stone was placed to represent the dead person. The relatives tended the grave, and in their prayers they called the soul of the dead person home.

Etruscan Necropolises

The Etruscans, who lived in northern Italy in the sixth century BCE, buried their relatives in special "cities of the dead," called necropolises. Whole streets of tombs were erected, each one a small houselike structure. Inside were marble coffins for the dead. There were also stone benches where people could sit and pray for their departed relatives.

▶ This cenotaph in Athens is marked by a special water jug called a lutrophoros, signifying the death of an unmarried man.

THE MAUSOLEUM AT HALICARNASSUS

The Mausoleum at Halicarnassus (present-day Bodrum in Turkey), built in 350 BCE, was the tomb of King Mausolus of Caria. Erected by his wife, Artemisia, the stone and marble tomb stood 148 feet (45 m) high and was one of the Seven Wonders of the Ancient World. It was a rectangular building, surrounded by columns and decorated with statues carved by the finest Greek sculptors of the time. The carvings included figures of people, lions, horses, and other animals. Inside the burial chamber lay the king's sarcophagus, made of pure alabaster and decorated with gold.

The magnificent tomb remained standing for sixteen centuries, until a minor earthquake destroyed part of the roof and some of the columns. Early in the fifteenth century, the tomb was dismantled, and the stone and marble were used to build a nearby castle. However, King Mausolus's memory still survives: the word mausoleum entered the English language to mean a large, ornate tomb.

▲ *The original frescoed decoration still survives in the second-century-CE Roman catacombs of Saint Januarius in Naples, southern Italy.*

The walls of Etruscan necropolises were decorated with frescoes showing scenes from Etruscan life such as banquets, dancing, and chariot racing. The Etruscans staged elaborate funerals involving special funeral games, such as juggling and throwing disks into a bucket.

Roman Burial

Like the Greeks, the ancient Romans sometimes burned their dead and buried the ashes in urns. The burial of whole corpses, however, became much more popular as the empire grew. The graves were either niches dug into walls or marble chambers built above ground. They were set along the roads leading into cities, perhaps to keep disease out of heavily populated areas. Graves were built close to the road itself so that travelers could see them and remember the dead inside. As space for new tombs became rare, the Romans copied the Etruscans, building vast underground cemeteries called catacombs.

With the conversion of the Romans to Christianity in the fourth century CE, the catacombs became places where the living commemorated not the death of their relatives but their entry into heaven. The graves were seen as symbols of heavenly homes, and the walls were decorated with images of people celebrating in heaven.

TOMBS WERE OFTEN INSCRIBED WITH COUNSEL TO THE LIVING.

This is the monument made to Marcus Caecilius. Guest, it is pleasing that you stopped at my place. May you run your affairs well and enjoy good health. May you sleep without care.

FROM AN INSCRIPTION ON A ROMAN TOMB, C. 140 BCE

SEE ALSO
- Archaeology • Christianity
- Death and Burial • Egypt • Etruscans
- Greece, Classical • Mummification
- Mycenaean Civilization • Prehistory
- Pyramids • Religion
- Roman Republic and Empire • Ur
- Valley of the Kings

Trade

The earliest trade presumably involved the simple exchange of one piece of naturally occurring stone or mineral for another. As civilizations grew, people began to trade food, building material, clothing, and whatever other natural resources their homeland provided. The growth of merchant enterprise during the second millennium BCE was a crucial factor in the development of civilization.

The First Trade

An important stage in the early development of towns and cities was the division of labor, with different people contributing different skills to the community. The majority worked on the land producing food. Others were engaged in tasks such as hunting, fishing, or the crafting of objects, such as pots. The exchange of goods between these groups—grain for fish or for a manufactured article, for example—was the first true trade.

Evidence from very early history suggests long-distance trade between the coast and inland. For instance, decorative seashells have been found at Çatal Hüyük in modern Turkey, an inland town that emerged in the seventh millennium BCE. Over time states began to emerge, and from the second millennium BCE, trade expanded in volume and distance.

The Goods of Trade

Sometimes a nation specialized in certain products specifically to trade them for objects from somewhere else. For example, ancient Egypt produced a huge surplus of grain, grown along the fertile banks of the Nile River. This grain would be traded with the lands of the eastern Mediterranean for timber, spices, oil, and other luxuries Egypt lacked.

In fact, since the Egyptians believed all other peoples were inferior to them, they did not refer to the exchange of goods as trade. Instead, they maintained that they were being paid tribute. A similar outlook existed among the Chinese.

◀ This ancient Egyptian model of a grain store, watched over by a workman and a bookkeeper, dates from around 1800 BCE.

The most common commodity of international trade was food. However, fresh goods, such as fish and meat, perished on long journeys. There were two ways of overcoming this problem. Animals, such as sheep or goats, either would be moved as living beasts or else would be slaughtered, and the meat dried and salted. Heavier goods, such as cereals and wine, had to be transported by water. Vast quantities of grain (rice, barley, wheat, rye, and oats) were carried along rivers and across the seas, especially the eastern Mediterranean.

Slaves, another popular trading commodity, could be transported by land or sea. The same applied to metals, although it was easier to take large quantities by ship. The most common form of land transport was the donkey or mule, often traveling in caravans of fifty beasts or more. In desert areas the camel was used.

Food, timber, and other necessities were frequently exchanged for luxuries. These included natural products, such as exotic animal skins, oils, spices, jewels, and scented or decorative woods. Just as important were manufactured goods of great beauty, such as silks, carpets, ornaments, jewelry, and lacquer work. The most famous route for such products—indeed, the most famous trade route in the ancient world—was the Silk Road. It ran west from central China, north of the Himalayas, south of the Caspian Sea to Asia Minor and finally to the cities of the eastern Mediterranean.

The First Merchants

With the exception of Egypt, where all trade was theoretically controlled by the pharaoh, the buying and selling of goods was in the hands of merchants—although Egypt had merchants, too. The emergence of the merchant classes was extremely important for the development of civilization. Merchants earned a living by their wits and daring rather than by making or growing things. They may fairly be called the first entrepreneurs.

Merchant enterprise stimulated a host of other developments. To beat the competition, merchants needed bigger and safer ships, better roads and bridges, and more and better quality goods to buy and sell.

The quest for new markets and sources of supply made merchants into explorers. Traders from the Mediterranean, for instance, had sailed north to Britain in search of tin long before Julius Caesar crossed to the island from France in 55 BCE.

To make their work easier, merchants encouraged the development of money. Literate and intelligent, they played a key role in the spread of ideas and understanding. Successful merchants used their profits to fund grand houses, works of art, and even whole cities and royal campaigns. In short, much of the wealth of the ancient world was generated not by its kings, princes and princesses but by its more humble merchants and traders.

THE LAWS OF THE BABYLONIAN KING HAMMURABI IN THE EIGHTEENTH CENTURY BCE CONTAIN SEVERAL CLAUSES DEALING WITH TRADE DISPUTES:

Law No. 102:

If a merchant leaves money with a broker for some investment, and the broker loses some or all of the money on his travels, he shall make good the loss to the merchant.

Law No. 104:

If a merchant gives an agent corn, wool, oil, or any other goods to transport, the agent shall give a receipt for what he has received and make sure that the merchant gets true value in return.

CODE OF HAMMURABI

◀ A nineteenth-century artist's impression of Phoenician merchants haggling over the prices of goods.

SEE ALSO

- Babylonians
- Çatal Hüyük
- Dunhuang
- Egypt • Money
- Transportation
- Weights and Measures

Transportation

For tens of thousands of years, walking was the only means by which people moved from one place to another. The earliest people found ways to make traveling on foot easier—by using snowshoes and skies in snowbound areas, for example. Not long after ancient peoples started to domesticate animals, they began to use them as a means of transport. By later ancient times, people had developed numerous ingenious methods of transportation, both on land and on water.

Although this oil painting of a caravan in Algeria dates from the nineteenth century, transportation methods in many parts of Africa and Asia had changed very little since ancient times.

Transportation Using Animals

At first beasts of burden, such as oxen and horses, were used to drag goods along behind them. Only later did people ride on an animal's back. In both eastern and western Asia, camels, with their great stamina and hardiness, became prized as transporters of people and goods.

In South America the llama, a relative of the camel, was domesticated around five thousand years ago. The ancient Maya used llamas to carry small cargoes, although they were not strong enough to carry an adult rider. Native North Americans had no camels or horses; they used large dogs bred from wolves to drag a travois, a triangular frame of wood on which were placed loads that weighed up to one hundred pounds (45 kg).

Early Water Transport

At least 11,000 years ago, Stone Age peoples in many places learned to use materials that float, such as wood and bundles of

NAVIGATION AT SEA

The development of faster, stronger ships enabled people to travel longer distances. As sailors ventured farther from land, it became more important for them to know which way their vessel was heading. While sailing close to shore, navigation was possible by recognizing landmarks, but when sailing across large stretches of water or at night, different methods were required.

At night stars rise in the east and set in the west. By carefully noting the positions of stars, many different civilizations, including the Polynesians, ancient Chinese, and Phoenicians, were able to work out the direction they were heading. The peoples of the Pacific were especially skilled at watching for particular species of birds and fish to tell them how close they were to land.

Other natural phenomena such as water currents and wind directions were also studied. In the Mediterranean, for instance, it was possible to tell the difference between the cold wind from the north and the warm south wind. A wind rose, a diagram showing the direction of eight major winds, is believed to have been invented by the Etruscans around the sixth century BCE.

The magnetic compass was invented by the Chinese in the first century CE. They discovered that a magnetic iron needle would point in a north-south line if floated in water on a sliver of wood. The compass became an invaluable aid to navigators.

reeds. The earliest boats may have been little more than a tree trunk that people sat on or used as a float. Later, a number of logs were lashed together with vines or plant fibers to make a simple raft. By 7400 BCE, stone tools (which were later replaced by iron tools) were being used to hollow out tree trunks to form simple dugout canoes. The remains of ancient canoes have been found on all continents. In the expert hands of Pacific peoples such as the Micronesians and Polynesians, these canoes were developed into sturdy, long-distance vessels that were capable of traveling distances of hundreds of miles.

◀ Known as the Hasholme log boat, this example of primitive water transport dates from around 500 BCE and was found in Yorkshire, England.

Boat and Ship Building

As tools and carpentry skills improved, larger boats and ships were built that could carry more people and goods and travel greater distances. In places where wood was not readily available, ancient peoples made use of other materials. The ancient Celts were among several peoples who made small round boats, called coracles, out of a frame of wicker covered with animal skins. By 7000 BCE the ancient Egyptians and Mesopotamians were using bundles of reeds lashed tightly together to build flat-bottomed boats for river transport.

Early boats drifted on river and sea currents or were powered by human hands using a paddle or oar. Simple square sails fitted to an upright wooden post, called a mast, were found on some Asian and Egyptian boats and ships by 3000 BCE. At some point between 300 and 100 BCE, the Chinese invented the rudder, which made it easier to steer a boat in a particular direction.

The Wheel

At some point in prehistory, humans learned that tree trunks and logs could be used as rollers to move heavy objects such as large rocks and stones across land. From these rollers (or perhaps from the potters wheel) came the most important transport invention of all: the wheel.

The first known examples of the wheel come from Mesopotamia and are at least five thousand years old. Early wheels were fitted to crude two- and four-wheeled wooden carts pulled by oxen or onagers (wild asses). As time passed, sections were carved out of the wood to reduce weight, and eventually spoked wooden wheels were in use. Nails made of copper or bronze studding the rims of early wheels helped them to last longer. The ancient Celts of northern Europe fitted wheels with a rim of iron to make them more durable—an innovation copied by other civilizations.

Wheeled Vehicles

Wheeled carts and wagons developed rapidly in many civilizations. The ancient Egyptians, Babylonians, and Assyrians were among the first to build fast, lightweight chariots for use in war. The ancient Chinese attached harnesses to horses and oxen so that they could pull covered carts carrying heavy loads of farm produce. The Romans

▼ A traditional Celtic coracle boat, with the internal framework of flexible tree branches bound together clearly visible.

PHOENICIAN BIREMES AND TRIREMES

The Phoenicians were among the finest sailors and builders of large ships in the ancient world. They established many harbors in the Mediterranean and traded with several nations. The Phoenicians were the first to build ships powered by two decks (biremes) or three decks (triremes) of oars. Some of these biremes and triremes fought in the earliest sea battles. These warships were sturdily built and featured as their main weapon a large wooden battering ram covered in bronze, which was used to punch a hole in the hulls of enemy ships. The Greeks, Persians, and Romans all copied Phoenician designs in the building of their own warships.

developed a range of wheeled vehicles suitable for use on the flat, well-drained Roman roads that linked the far reaches of their empire together. One of their largest vehicles was the *clabularium*. Capable of carrying loads up to 1,100 pounds (500 kg), it was pulled by eight oxen and used to ferry supplies to the Roman armies.

◀ This Chinese bronze sculpture of a two-wheeled cart with a large parasol to protect the driver from the elements dates back approximately 2,200 years to the Eastern Han dynasty.

SEE ALSO
- Geography
- Micronesian Culture
- Phoenicians
- Polynesian Culture
- Roads
- Ships and Boats
- Technology
- Trade

Troy

Troy was a fabled city even during the times of classical Greece and the Roman Empire. Its true location was unknown until the nineteenth century, when it was traced to Hissarlik, a site in present-day Turkey. The Trojan War, probably fought around 1184 BCE between the city of Troy and an alliance of Greek kings led by Agamemnon, is the subject of Homer's *Iliad*.

The Trojan War

According to the *Iliad*, the Trojan War lasted for ten years. It started when Paris, son of the Trojan king Priam, won the love of Helen and abducted her from her husband, Menelaus, king of the Greek city-state of Sparta.

A fleet of Greek ships sailed to Troy to win back Helen. After a long siege and dreadful losses on both sides, the Greeks used a much-celebrated trick. They left a large wooden horse outside the walls of Troy and sailed away, apparently defeated. The Trojans, thinking the horse was a gift, took it inside.

During the night, as the Trojans celebrated their victory, Greek soldiers, who had been hiding inside the horse, crept out and opened the gates for their returning army, which burned Troy to the ground.

The story of the Trojan War captivated later Greeks and Romans. Both Alexander the Great and Julius Caesar visited the site for inspiration. Sometime after 550 CE, however, the site ceased to be inhabited, and Troy was soon lost under many layers of earth.

The Search for Troy

In the 1860s, archaeologists believed they had discovered Troy at the mound of Hissarlik (a Turkish name that means "the place of the fort"). Excavations at Hissarlik have uncovered ten different strata (layers)

▶ The eastern walls of Troy VI, excavated by Carl Blegen in 1938. The low walls in the foreground are the remains of the eastern defensive tower, which jutted out from the main wall and allowed Trojan archers to fire in all directions on their attackers.

◄ This clay storage jar, which dates from around 675 BCE, shows wide-eyed Greek soldiers hiding inside the Trojan horse, waiting to spring out and attack the unsuspecting Trojans.

of remains, the strata indicating that the settlement was rebuilt at least nine times. The earliest level, known as Troy 0, dates to before 3000 BCE, and the most recent, Troy IX, was abandoned around 550 CE.

Troy VI (1500–1275 BCE) flourished around the traditional date of the Trojan War. Much larger than the earlier settlements, it was protected by high limestone walls angled at the bottom, the description matching that of Troy in the *Iliad*.

Evidence shows that Troy VI was damaged by an earthquake and rebuilt (Troy VIIa). In this layer there is evidence of a long siege and also signs of destruction: ashes, crushed bodies, and an arrowhead. Carl Blegen, the German archaeologist who excavated Troy VIIa in the 1930s, was convinced he had found evidence for the sacking of Troy, which he dated to around 1250 BCE.

Troy remains one of the world's most controversial archaeological sites. Heinrich Schliemann, the first person to carry out major excavations, was criticized for destroying evidence in his haste to prove Hissarlik was Troy. Some also accused him of planting finds for dramatic effect.

HECTOR

Hector was the eldest son of King Priam and the bravest Trojan hero. He first appears in the *Iliad* leading the Trojans into battle, and he fights valiantly during the siege.

In battle, Hector kills Patroclus, a great friend of the Greek hero Achilles. Mad with grief, Achilles kills Hector and carries out a shameful revenge. He ties Hector's body to his chariot and drags it around the city walls until it is mutilated. King Priam is forced to pay a ransom to the Greeks for the release of his son's body. The *Iliad* ends with Hector's funeral.

SEE ALSO

- Agamemnon • Archaeology • Greece, Classical
- Greek Mythology • Iliad and Odyssey

Trung Sisters

In the first century CE Vietnam was a Chinese province named Giao Chi. Trung Trac and Trung Nhi, the two daughters of a local Vietnamese leader, led an uprising that for a short period drove the Chinese out of their country. Their deeds are remembered and celebrated to this day by the people of Vietnam.

Chinese Occupation

Vietnam had been occupied and controlled by its powerful neighbor China since 111 BCE. Successive Chinese governors of Giao Chi caused discontent among the population by levying large taxes. Matters were made worse by the arrival, in 36 CE, of Su Ting, a particularly brutal and greedy governor. He insisted on being paid bribes and imposed taxes on salt and even on fish caught in local rivers. Trung Trac and Trung Nhi grew up in the Me Linh area of Vietnam and witnessed at close hand the cruel Chinese treatment of their people. In private they studied the arts of warfare and honed their fighting skills.

A Call to Arms

At the age of nineteen, the elder of the two sisters, Trung Trac, married Dang Thi Sach, the son of a leader of Chu Dien, a neighboring area of Vietnam. Dang Thi Sach was also extremely resentful of the Chinese domination. He and his new wife, along with her sister, started to prepare an uprising among the local Vietnamese. In 39 CE the governor, Su Ting, ordered the arrest and imprisonment of Dang Thi Sach for complaining about the high taxes. Shortly afterward, Dang Thi Sach was executed and his body displayed publicly. What was meant as a warning to the Vietnamese people became a rallying call to arms.

▶ In rural Vietnam, people fish using much the same methods as were used in the time of the Trung sisters.

Rebellion

Trung Trac took overall command of the uprising, while Trung Nhi traveled throughout Vietnam building support and recruiting soldiers. In June 40 CE Trung Trac addressed some 30,000 Vietnamese male and female soldiers and declared war on the Han dynasty of China. Their success was startling. Before the end of 40 CE, the Chinese were driven out of most of Vietnam. Supported by the rejoicing Vietnamese people, Trung Trac was crowned queen of Vietnam. After setting up her capital in her local area of Me Linh, her government removed many of the loathed heavy taxes and tried to create a simpler, fairer way of ruling the country.

Defeat and Retreat

The victory was short-lived. Within three years, China regrouped and sent large forces led by one of its most capable and experienced generals, Ma Yuan. The Chinese invaded Vietnam and fought the Trung sisters' forces at Lang Bac. Outnumbered by the Chinese and often fighting with inferior weapons, the Vietnamese were defeated there and in several other battles. Retreating to the Hat Giang River, the weakened armies of the Trungs suffered a final, crushing defeat. On February 6, 43 CE, rather than be captured, the two sisters committed suicide in the traditional manner of Vietnamese nobles: they drowned themselves in the Hat Giang River. Chinese rule was restored, but the sisters remain national heroines to this day. Vietnamese women and men continue to honor them on Hai Ba Trung day in March.

SEE ALSO
• China

▼ *Throughout Vietnam shrines are dedicated to the Trung Sisters, and one day a year is set aside for the Hai Ba Trung Festival.*

THE FOLLOWING IS PART OF TRUNG TRAC'S ADDRESS TO THE FORCES GATHERED IN JUNE 40 CE TO FIGHT THE CHINESE:

First, I will avenge my country,
Second, I will restore the Hung lineage,
Third, I will avenge the death of my husband,
Lastly, I vow that these goals will be accomplished.

Tutankhamen

Born in about 1345 BCE, Tutankhamen ruled Egypt from around 1336 to 1327 BCE. He was almost certainly a son of Akhenaten by his minor wife Kiya. Tutankhamen was brought up in Amarna, his father's capital city, and taught to worship one god, Aten. His original name, Tutankhaten, contained that god's name, as did the names of all royal children. While still a young child, he was married to his half sister, Ankhesenpaaten, the daughter of Akhenaten and Nefertiti.

▼ *This gold mask was placed over the head of Tutankhamen's mummy when he was buried.*

Tutankhamen did not rule immediately after his father; at first, a pharaoh named Smenkhkare ruled for a short time. Because there is so little historical evidence, nothing is known about Smenkhkare. Egyptologists do not even know if Smenkhkare was male or female.

The Young Pharaoh

In 1336 BCE Tutankhamen became pharaoh. Following the upheaval of Akhenaten's reign, Egypt needed a strong ruler. As the new pharaoh was just nine years old, the country was run by a regent, an adult from the royal family who ruled until the pharaoh could rule for himself. In Tutankhamen's case, Ay, who had been a close adviser of Akhenaten, seems to have acted as regent, supported by the military commander Horemheb.

An Early Death

Tutankhamen died in 1327 BCE, at about the age of twenty, a time when he should have started ruling for himself. His death is a mystery. He certainly died suddenly and was buried in a small tomb in the Valley of the Kings probably built for Ay. When his mummy was unwrapped, it showed signs of having been overtreated with embalming resins, which had been used in such generous quantities that the mummy was stuck

to the wooden mummy case. The archaeologists damaged the body unwrapping it, but at least one piece of damage, a blow to the head, happened in ancient times and could have been what killed Tutankhamen. There is no way of knowing if the blow was an accident or if Tutankhamen was murdered by Ay, who took over as pharaoh.

A Famous Pharaoh

Tutankhamen's life was short, and almost nothing is known about it. Yet he is one of the most famous of the Egyptian pharaohs, mainly because his tomb was found virtually intact with almost all of its treasures still in place. Its rich and fascinating contents were discovered by the archaeologist Howard Carter and his team in November 1922.

HOWARD CARTER *1874–1939*

Howard Carter was an archaeologist who discovered the tombs of several Egyptian pharaohs. When most people believed that all the tombs had been found, Carter was convinced that Tutankhamen's tomb lay undiscovered in the Valley of the Kings. He persuaded his longtime sponsor, Lord Carnarvon, to pay for additional excavation and began his search in 1917.

After five years, Carter had still not found the tomb or anything else of great financial value. Carnarvon wanted to give up, but Carter begged for one more try. He began digging again in November 1922. Three days later the search team found steps in the sand. By the end of the week, they had reached a door with Tutankhamen's name on it. Carnarvon was sent for, and when he arrived, they made a hole into the first room of the tomb. Carter put a candle through the opening and looked through. When Carnarvon impatiently asked what Carter could see, there was a long pause before Carter said, "Wonderful things." He spent most of the rest of his life working on the treasures he had found.

SEE ALSO

• Egypt • Egyptian Mythology • Nefertiti
• Thebes • Valley of the Kings

Tyre

The Phoenician city of Tyre was founded in about 2000 BCE on islets of rock off the coast of Lebanon, twelve miles (19 km) north of the present-day border with Israel. Although Tyre was under the control of other empires for most of its history, it nevertheless became a wealthy seafaring city-state.

History

Until the twelfth century BCE, Tyre was a semi-independent city in the Syrian part of the Egyptian Empire. It grew in importance after 1000 BCE under the Phoenician king Hiram. The Tyrians became excellent sailors and built ships with keels, which were more dependable in bad weather.

In the ninth century BCE, Tyre established colonies around the Mediterranean, including Carthage on the North African coast. However, at about this time the rising power of Assyria conquered Tyre. Dominating the city for the next two centuries, the Assyrians exacted tribute from the Tyrians in exchange for their freedom. However, because of its island location, Tyre was difficult to conquer entirely. On several occasions the Assyrians and later the Babylonians besieged Tyre for years at a time but failed to defeat the city.

In the sixth century BCE, Tyre was incorporated into the new Persian Empire and grew rich on the empire's trade. Tyre's ships provided the Persians with fleets for the invasion of Egypt and Greece.

In 332 BCE Tyre faced its gravest threat when Alexander the Great demanded to be allowed into the city to worship the god Melqart. The Tyrians refused, and

▶ The ruins of ancient Tyre in Lebanon, with the port of Tyre in the background.

Alexander's army destroyed the entire mainland part of the city and used the rubble to create a causeway out to the island part. After months of war, Tyre fell, all its citizens were killed or sold into slavery, and the city was razed to the ground. Tyre, however, was reoccupied and rebuilt and flourished once again, first in the empire of the Seleucids and from 64 BCE in the Roman Empire. By the second century CE, Tyre had a large Christian community, and by the fifth century, its language had died out and been replaced by Aramaic.

Religion

The chief god of Tyre was Melqart, known by the title Ruler of the City. The entrance to Tyre's temple to Melqart contained two pillars, one of emerald and one of gold. Temples, like other public buildings in Tyre, were built of stone and had a central courtyard surrounded by single-story rooms. The temple had a central block housing the shrine of the god.

JEZEBEL

In 875 BCE Jezebel, the daughter of the king of Tyre, married Ahab, the ruler of Israel. Ahab was madly in love with Jezebel and did whatever she told him. Jezebel brought her worship of the god Melqart to Jerusalem and began persecuting and killing the prophets of the Israelite god Yahweh. The prophet Elijah led a rebellion against her. She was thrown out of her bedroom window, and her body was eaten by wild dogs.

Commerce

At its height, Tyre was a thriving center of industry. It had a glass factory where transparent blown glass was mass produced. The city also produced an expensive purple dye, made from a sea snail, that was used to color the cloaks and togas of Greek and Roman kings and emperors. Other Tyre workshops produced carved ivory, jewelry, iron and bronze weapons, and dark red pottery. In Roman times a hippodrome (a stadium used for chariot races) was built at Tyre, as well as public baths and a necropolis.

SEE ALSO

- Alexander the Great
- Assyrians
- Babylonians
- Carthage
- Phoenicians

Uluru

Over 190 miles (300 km) southwest of Alice Springs in Australia's Northern Territory lies a massive rocky outcrop made of sandstone. Named Ayers Rock in the nineteenth century by European settlers in Australia, it is now also known once again by its traditional aboriginal name, Uluru. It is a site of enormous importance to the local peoples, who have lived around the rock for thousands of years.

Covering an area of approximately 1.25 square miles (3.3 km²), the huge monolithic rock of Uluru stands out against the surrounding flat scrubland.

Focal Point

Uluru is 1,142 feet (348 m) high with a circumference of 5.9 miles (9.4 km). It is believed to have orginated as sediment laid down in a shallow inland sea known as the Amadeus Basin. More than 300 million years ago, the sediments were forced up above sea level.

Aborigines reached Australia at least 40,000 years ago, but no one is certain when they first reached and settled the area around Uluru. The earliest signs of aboriginal life at Uluru date from 10,000 years ago. Two of the local groups for which Uluru provided a focal point, the Pitjantjatjara and Yankunytjatjara people (also known as the Anangu), still live in the area.

Sacred Site

According to aboriginal dreamtime beliefs, the world existed before dreamtime but was featureless. The ancestral beings (giant semihumans) rose up and began to roam the land. As they wandered, they carried out tasks such as camping and digging for water and fought with one another. Some form of natural feature now marks each place where the creators were active.

ULURU ART

The caves around the base of Uluru contain many examples of aboriginal art. On their walls can be found hundreds of paintings and carvings depicting aboriginal life. Many of them have great significance to the present-day aboriginal community and are out of bounds to nonaboriginals. Most were originally painted using a simple brush made by chewing one end of a piece of tree bark so that it frayed into strands. This brush was dipped into colored pastes made by grinding red and yellow ochers and white pipe clay. Charcoal was used to provide black coloring.

◀ A face carved in the side of Uluru, one of many parts of the giant rock that is sacred to local aboriginal peoples.

There are many such features on and around Uluru, which aborigines believe was the work of two ancestral beings, young boys, piling up mud to form a monolith. Certain caves in the rock are seen as the open mouths of warriors who died shouting at their enemies. Another is the open mouth of a grieving mother who saw her son being killed. She avenged his death by striking a warrior. His cracked skull, with four holes representing his eyes and nasal passages, can be seen on the rock along with his blood (water stains).

Uluru also features a water hole, and all water holes are considered sacred, as they give life to people, animals, and plants. There is also a birthing cave in the rock, a place where pregnant women went in the belief they would have a painless delivery during childbirth.

Climbing Uluru is an important *inma* (ritual) for aborigines, as it involves retracing the path taken by ancestral beings to the summit. It is a privilege that only a handful of aboriginal males get the opportunity to perform.

SEE ALSO
• Aboriginal Culture
• Kakadu Region

Ur

Ur, an important city of Sumer, was located in southern Mesopotamia (in present-day Iraq), close to a tributary of the Euphrates River. The Euphrates provided Ur with access to the sea, a crucial factor in its success as a center of trade. Archaeological discoveries of the 1920s and 1930s were very important in establishing the city's historical significance.

A list of Sumerians kings, probably compiled around 2100 BCE, mentions three dynasties, but most of what archaeologists know about Ur comes from the periods of the first and third dynasties. The first began around 2400 BCE, and the third, founded by King Ur-Nammu, began around 2100 BCE. The third dynasty lasted only a century but saw the creation of a centralized state that ruled a large part of Mesopotamia, as had the Akkadian empire between around 2340 and 2150 BCE.

Royal Graves

In the 1920s a joint British-U.S. team excavating the site of Ur made spectacular finds in the cemetery area: a set of sixteen tombs was found, dating from the period before the first dynasty. These tombs were identified as royal graves because of the wealth of precious objects buried with the bodies. The tombs held funeral goods made from every precious material available at the time—gold, silver, ivory, precious stones, copper, and bronze. Buried with these

▼ *This Sumerian necklace, measuring sixteen inches (41 cm), is made of gold and lapis lazuli (a shiny blue mineral).*

Found in one of the royal graves at Ur and dating from around 2500 BCE, this model of a ram feeding at a bush is a symbol of fertility.

high-ranking people were the bodies of servants and court officials, who were long considered by scholars to have been sacrificed but are now thought to have died a natural death and to have chosen to stay close to those they had served.

Women were adorned with fine ornaments and valuable jewelry such as silver and gold earrings and chokerlike necklaces, and men with well-crafted weapons, including daggers, knives, and axes, and headdresses made of gold. The skill of Sumerian craftspeople is evident in the elaborate detailing on many of these objects. The wealth displayed in these tombs gives an indication of the great prosperity enjoyed by this Sumerian city, as well as the high development of its art and civilization.

THE ZIGGURAT OF UR-NAMMU

Ziggurats—temples shaped like stepped pyramids—were built in several Mesopotamian cities. The best-preserved example of a ziggurat is the one that Ur-Nammu began building at Ur; it was completed by his son, Shulgi. Restoration work carried out in the late 1970s brought many of its most impressive features to light.

The ziggurat rose on three levels from a platform, each level smaller than the one below. Only part of the second level remains, and it is not known if a temple stood on the top level. The core of the ziggurat was made from mud bricks. The outer walls were covered with bitumen to protect it from the climate, and drainage pipes were added to keep the structure dry.

Ur-Nammu's ziggurat was a massive building that would have dominated the skyline of the city, rising high above the walls surrounding it, as well as the walls of Ur itself. It is not known for certain how the ziggurat was used in Ur. According to one theory, ziggurats were used as platforms from which to make astronomical observations. It is also likely that public celebrations took place and rituals were performed on the ziggurat.

SEE ALSO
- Akkadians
- Mesopotamia
- Shulgi
- Sumer

Valley of the Kings

The Valley of the Kings is situated at the edge of the desert on the west bank of the Nile River, opposite the modern city of Luxor, which stands where the ancient city of Thebes once stood. In the Valley of the Kings, tunnels were cut deep into the rock face to make tombs for the pharaohs of Egypt. The earliest tomb dates from around 1504 BCE (although tombs in the nearby hills date from around 2200 BCE). Nearby is the Valley of the Queens, where the wives and sons of some of the pharaohs were buried.

A Secret Place

The New Kingdom pharaohs, who ruled until 1069 BCE, chose the Valley of the Kings as a burial site for several reasons. It was close to their capital city, Thebes. It was also, they hoped, isolated enough for their tombs to remain hidden. Earlier pharaohs had been buried in pyramids—very visible signs of power and importance—and had relied on careful building, with thick walls, traps, and dead ends, to keep tombs and occupants safe from grave robbers. The New Kingdom pharaohs knew that their predecessors' precautions had failed: the pyramids and the mummified bodies had been robbed. Thus, the only visible sign of the tombs in the Valley of the Kings was a small entrance in a cliff that was watched by a special police service. Another important reason for choosing the valley was that it lies beneath a rock shaped naturally like a pyramid.

Tomb Robbers

Despite all the efforts of the pharaohs to keep their burial places secret, most tombs

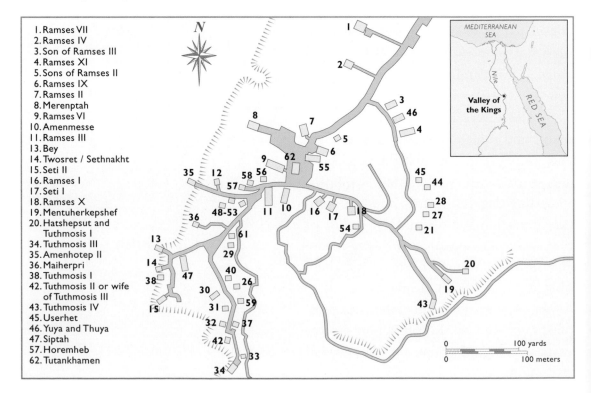

1. Ramses VII
2. Ramses IV
3. Son of Ramses III
4. Ramses XI
5. Sons of Ramses II
6. Ramses IX
7. Ramses II
8. Merenptah
9. Ramses VI
10. Amenmesse
11. Ramses III
13. Bey
14. Twosret / Sethnakht
15. Seti II
16. Ramses I
17. Seti I
18. Ramses X
19. Mentuherkepshef
20. Hatshepsut and Tuthmosis I
34. Tuthmosis III
35. Amenhotep II
36. Maiherpri
38. Tuthmosis I
42. Tuthmosis II or wife of Tuthmosis III
43. Tuthmosis IV
45. Userhet
46. Yuya and Thuya
47. Siptah
57. Horemheb
62. Tutankhamen

▶ This map shows the location of all the major tombs in the Valley of the Kings.

THE TOMB BUILDERS

The tomb builders of the Valley of the Kings lived in the village of Deir el-Medina. Unlike most other ancient Egyptian settlements, Deir el-Medina was built in the desert, rather than beside the banks of the Nile River, so that the workers would be near the Valley of the Kings. Everything they needed, including food and water, had to be brought to the village on donkeys.

Deir el-Medina was a mud-brick village, initially containing about seventy houses for the workers and their families. Each of the workers' homes had around four rooms and stairs to a flat roof, where much of the cooking and housework was done. The officials who ran Deir el-Medina had larger houses.

The workers, who included stonemasons, carpenters, sculptors, and painters, lived in a camp beside the tombs. They worked for around eight days at a time and then had two days off. During these "weekends" and on festival days, they returned to their families in the village. Women did not work on the tombs but ran their homes. Their tasks included weaving cloth and brewing beer.

The workmen were paid not in coinage but in the provision of homes, clothes, and food for their families. If this payment was late, the workmen sometimes went on strike: the first recorded workers' strike in history occurred at Deir el-Medina. In their spare time the villagers built themselves tombs in the cliffs behind the village. These tombs were much smaller than the royal tombs, but they were just as beautifully decorated.

were discovered and robbed in ancient times. Sometimes tomb builders themselves and even corrupt high officials were tempted to steal from the tombs or to accept bribes from gangs of tomb robbers. Pharaohs and their officials seldom lay undisturbed in the Valley of the Kings.

▶ Thousands of tourists visiting the Valley of the Kings each year find out for themselves how difficult it is to spot the tomb entrances.

Reburied Mummies

In 1881 archaeologists discovered a tomb containing over fifty mummies that obviously had been reburied. They worked out that this reburying was done in ancient times but after the New Kingdom period.

Labels from the time of reburial told the archaeologists that they had found a group of pharaohs, queens, and officials. They had been reburied together in this way because it was easier for the official guards in the Valley of the Kings to watch one tomb than fifty or more.

In 1891 and again in 1898, two more groups of mummies, many of them royal, were found reburied, presumably for the same reasons. Some of the mummies had been rewrapped before they were reburied. Their original tombs had been robbed and their wrappings torn open so that the thieves could get at the valuable amulets placed within the wrappings.

AMENPANUFER *C. 1124–1108 BCE*

Amenpanufer was the leader of a gang of tomb robbers who operated in the Valley of the Kings in the twelfth century BCE. In 1108 the gang was questioned about the robbery of the tomb of the pharaoh Sobekemsaf II. Amenpanufer confessed to being the gang leader and to planning the robbery of the tomb. The reports on the trial suggest that some important officials, including the mayors of the east and west banks of the Nile River at Thebes, were involved in the robbery. The gang was sentenced to death. Stealing from tombs was seen as such a serious crime that tomb robbers were executed by being impaled: pushed down onto a long sharpened pole and left to die.

▼ *This painted ceiling from the tomb of Ramses VI (reigned 1143–1136 BCE) shows the journey of the sun, which the goddess Nut swallows at night and gives birth to in the morning.*

Warfare and Conquest

War, that is, large-scale conflict involving organized armies, appeared at the very dawn of civilization. Sadly, people were fighting each other long before they learned to write or built the first towns. In fact, some of the ancient world's oldest civilized remains—the walls of Jericho (c. 6000 BCE), for instance—are associated with conflict.

Causes of War

The principal cause of war has always been the desire of civilizations to expand their territory or to resist the expansion of other civilizations into their territory. The underlying causes include greed, pride, superstition, revenge, fear, and misunderstanding, any of which might set one people against another. The wealthy Chinese and Roman Empires were subjected to almost continual attacks from poorer peoples living beyond their frontiers. The extraordinary conquests of Alexander the Great (356–323 BCE), perhaps the greatest warrior general of all time, were fired by a desire to take revenge on the Persians for their attacks on Greece. The momentum of Alexander's remarkable campaign was due in no small part to his great pride.

Religious differences frequently sparked conflict between rival powers. The role of religion in warfare is clear, for example, from the history of the Jewish people as recorded in the Old Testament. Indeed, of all the major ancient religions, only one—Buddhism—specifically condemned the use of force.

Weapons

In 6000 BCE, as the first civilizations were emerging, the range of military weapons was limited to slings, bows and arrows, wooden spears, and clubs. Stone, especially flint, was often bound to the wood to give greater weight and sharpness. Copper weapons first appeared around 3500 BCE, and tougher bronze weapons several hundreds years later

▼ *This bronze helmet from Corinth, Greece, dates from around the sixth century BCE.*

During the Bronze and Iron Ages, the major developments were the sword and armor (a covering of metal plates to protect the body). By the end of ancient times, armor had become very sophisticated, with coats of steel rings (chain mail) being worn by both people and horses.

Chariots and Cavalry

Horse-drawn war chariots were first employed in Sumer around 2500 BCE, the Chinese developing them shortly afterward. These terrifying war machines dominated most battlefields until about the sixth century BCE. In India the equivalent of the chariot, the elephant, carried up to six archers. Hannibal, the Carthaginian general, famously used war elephants in his invasion of Italy in 218 BCE.

The Assyrians were the first to use cavalry effectively (around 1000 BCE). Cavalry played an important role in European conflicts, although the Greeks and especially the Romans based their armies around the infantry. Roman infantry legions, well organized and armed with large shields and short swords, were among the most effective soldiers ever seen.

By 400 CE the dominance of the Roman legion had been replaced by that of the heavy cavalry. Horsemen had always been more important in Asia, where one of the key inventions of the period emerged—the saddle with stirrups. This innovation turned the horse into a stable fighting platform on which the rider could wield sword, lance, or bow and arrow with ease.

Sea, Siege, and Strategy

The first warships were built by the Phoenicians around 700 BCE, and the designs were later improved by the Greeks and Romans. Driven by sails or banks of oars and armed with catapults, rams, and grappling hooks, the warships of this period were spectacular fighting vessels.

By 200 CE the art of defense and siege was well advanced. The world's most famous defensive construction, the Great Wall of China, was started in 214 BCE and

▶ *This fifteenth-century-CE tapestry of the Roman victory over Carthage at the Battle of Zama (202 BCE) captures the chaos of war if not the dreadful noise.*

added to for 1500 years. At the same time, the siege engineers of the great civilizations were producing rams, giant catapults, and wheeled castles to break through enemy defenses.

People also made great advances in the theory and organization of war. Generals learned how best to combine infantry and cavalry. The importance of supply was recognized. The Romans and Chinese, in particular, set great store by training and discipline.

The Egyptians were perhaps the first to study military strategy and tactics. Additional developments were made by the Assyrians and Persians. The period between 400 and 200 BCE saw the most remarkable flowering of military thinking. Among its geniuses were Alexander the Great, Hannibal, Scipio Africanus, Chandragupta Maurya, and Cheng. The greatest work of military theory was Sun Tzu's *The Art of War*, which was written in the fifth century BCE and is still studied.

JULIUS CAESAR DESCRIBES THE MILITARY TACTICS OF THE BRITONS, WHO FOUGHT FROM CHARIOTS:

First they ride all over the field hurling missiles, and the terrifying horses and clatter of wheels is usually enough to confound the enemy. When they have worked their way among the squadrons of their own cavalry they leap down from their chariots and fight on foot. Meanwhile the drivers gradually withdraw from the battle and park their vehicles in such a way that if their charioteers are hard pressed . . . they will have an easy retreat to their own side. In action, therefore, they exhibit the mobility of cavalry and the steadiness of infantry.

JULIUS CAESAR, *GALLIC WAR*

SEE ALSO
- Alexander the Great • Assyrians • Caesar, Julius • Cheng • China
- Great Wall of China • Hannibal • Jericho • Phoenicians
- Roman Republic and Empire • Ships and Boats • Technology

Weights and Measures

In the modern world, people measure or weigh objects with devices such as rulers and scales and use units of measurement recognized all over the world, such as the inch, pound, meter, and kilogram. In prehistoric times, people had no way of weighing and measuring other than direct comparison between the size of one object and the size of another. As civilizations arose, systems of weights and measures were developed.

The First Measuring Units

Some early measures consisted of products of the natural world, such as seeds laid end to end, but the first practical systems of measurement used the human body to provide standard units. The ancient Egyptians, Greeks, and Romans all used hands and fingers. The basic unit of length in ancient Greece was the width of the finger, equal to three-quarters of an inch (19 mm), with sixteen fingers equaling a Greek foot. The ancient Egyptians used

▼ *This sixth-century-BCE Greek vase shows cloth merchants using balance scales to weigh bales of cloth.*

two hand measurements: the width of a palm and the width of a man's middle finger, called the digit. The Babylonians were the first civilization to use the human foot as a measuring unit, around 1500 BCE.

However, the most successful body measurement of the ancient world was the cubit. It originated in ancient Egypt around 3000 BCE and was based on the length of an adult's arm from the elbow to the extended fingertips. Because humans vary in size, a royal cubit was fashioned in ancient Egypt out of black granite. It measured twenty inches (54.2 cm) and was the standard against which all other cubit sticks in Egypt were checked. Over the centuries, use of the cubit spread throughout much of Europe and Asia.

Early Weighing Methods

Until the arrival of large-scale trade, the weight of goods was generally estimated by hand. Over time, the use of containers of a certain shape and size became customary in trade, such as a basket of plants or a vessel full of wine or grain. In ancient China, containers were struck with a stick, and the sound made was used to measure the contents, the pitch indicating how empty or full the container was.

ANCIENT WEIGHTS AND WEIGHING DEVICES

As people began to work metals, particularly precious metals, such as gold, there arose the need for accurate methods of weighing these substances. Historians believe the ancient Egyptians were the first people to use scales, as the earliest known weights, dating from around 3500 BCE, are Egyptian. The earliest scales consisted of two small pans hung on either end of a beam or pole. Gold, silver, or copper was placed in one pan and balanced against a set of weights placed in the other.

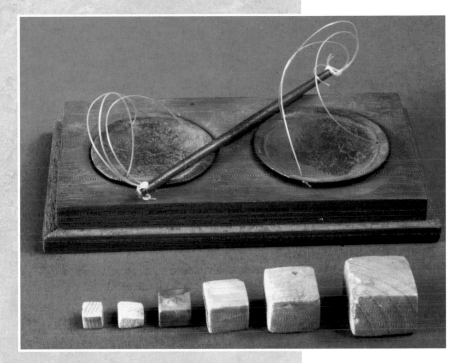

▲ This scale and set of weights, made of a type of quartz rock called chert, date from between 2300 and 1750 BCE and come from the Indus valley settlement of Mohenjo Daro.

Gradually the systems of weights used with scales became standardized within a region or throughout a civilization. One of the first-known standard weights was the mina, used in Babylonia by 2600 BCE. The mina weighed approximately two pounds, two ounces (970 g).

The ancient Egyptians made their weights out of bronze, stone, or pottery, often sculpted into models of animals or birds; civilizations in India, China, and Africa also fashioned weights in the shapes of creatures, frequently made of brass.

It became a crime in many civilizations to create false weights, which traders would use to cheat customers. In ancient Greece, for example, people were employed to check that the weights used in markets were fair. These officials were called metronomoi after the Greek word metron, meaning "to measure." They checked market traders' weights against their own standard set.

Ancient Egyptians are depcited using ropes to measure their plots of land in this wall painting, which was found in the tomb of the royal scribe Menna and dates from around 1380 BCE.

Measuring Distance

The accurate measurement of distance gradually grew in importance as empires expanded and rival claims were made to land and property. In ancient Egypt, farmers who worked the land next to the Nile River had to contend with annual flooding—which was vital for irrigation but which washed away the boundaries that separated their fields. Pieces of rope, twelve cubits long, with a knot tied every cubit, were used to measure and mark out the fields each new year. The ropes were carried by teams of men known as rope stretchers.

The Romans, whose measurements were based mostly on those used in ancient Greece, did invent a new measurement: the mile. The word comes from the Latin *mille*, meaning "one thousand." A Roman mile was a thousand paces long (each pace being two strides of a Roman soldier), a distance equivalent to 1,597 yards (1,460 m). The Romans rigorously enforced their standard system of weights and measures throughout their empire, but with the empire's fall, weights and measures became more localized until the arrival of the metric system in the eighteenth century CE.

STANDARDIZING WEIGHTS IN CHINA

Cheng became the first emperor of China in 221 BCE. One of his most notable achievements during his sixteen-year reign was to standardize many of the units of weight and measurement in China. The basic weight, known as the shih, or tan, was fixed at about 132 pounds (60 kg), and there were two basic units of measuring length: the chih, approximately 9.8 inches (25 cm), and the chang, which measured nine feet, nine inches (3 m).

SEE ALSO

- Babylonians • Cheng • Egypt
- Greece, Classical • Money • Numbers
- Roman Republic and Empire
- Science

Women

Ancient civilizations depended as much upon women as men for their survival and prosperity. In most societies the status of women was generally lower than that of men; still, no generalization applies to all cultures. In some societies a woman's place was highly structured, while in others it was more fluid. Whether functioning as goddesses or laborers, however, women played essential roles.

Goddesses

The earliest deity figures, dating from as long ago as 25,000 BCE, were female. Woman was seen as the producer of life, and female deities were associated with symbols of creation such as the sun and the spring.

Early shrines to such deities, known as earth goddesses or mother goddesses, have been found at Çatal Hüyük, Jericho, Hacilar, and Sumer. The Celts continued to worship an earth mother figure until they encountered Roman and Christian civilization. Among the aborigines of Australia and certain peoples of the Americas, earth goddesses survived into the modern era.

By the classical era, which began in Europe around 800 BCE, male gods, such as the Greek Zeus, had been raised into the highest position in most pantheons. There were, however, exceptions. The deity believed to preside over Athens, for some time the most important Greek city-state, was Athena, the goddess of war and of wisdom.

Priestesses

Most cults had male chief priests, although Egyptian high priestesses were, in some periods, second in authority only to the pharaoh. Of all the major religions except that of ancient Egypt, Buddhism held women in the highest regard. However, Buddhists regarded women as inferior to men.

▶ A pottery figure of an earth goddess, the source of all life, made in western Asia sometime around 5500 BCE.

A first-century-CE marble statue of Messalina, the wife of the Roman emperor Claudius. She is holding her son Britannicus.

Mistress of the Household

In early civilizations as in modern, the successful management of a family home depended on a division of labor. As bearers and raisers of children, women spent much time indoors, while a man's work lay outside the home, usually in the fields. The maternal role was an overarching factor in women's lives. From as young as twelve years old, many women spent much of their time caring for young children. This task put great physical restrictions on them.

Yet it seems that in the households of the great bulk of the population, the distinction between the work of women and the work of men was not so clearly drawn. Poor women not only managed the home, they also spun and wove cloth, made clothes, and in many cases worked beside their husband in the fields.

Women from wealthy families fulfilled the role of mistress of the household more exclusively. As manager of a large home and its team of servants, provider of frequent large feasts, and supervisor of a continual program of upkeep and repair, as well as mother to her children, the work of a wealthy woman was no less arduous than that of a poor woman. In ancient Greece women from wealthy families passed most of their life indoors.

Although wealthy women generally enjoyed a more comfortable life than poorer women, their lives were usually far more restricted. Wealthy women were expected to dress modestly (often with covered head) and not to leave the house unaccompanied by a male. Low-born women enjoyed greater freedom, especially before marriage. Most societies did not object to their doing manual labor, and they could also work as dancers, musicians, shopkeepers, and even as prostitutes.

Women in Society

There is evidence that until about 2000 BCE societies were matriarchal. That is to say, women held the governing authority in the family and in politics. Man's task was to feed a woman, guard her, and keep her happy, for without her there could be no future. However, over the centuries, all the great civilizations became patriarchal, that is, men came to hold the greater authority. By the Iron Age, in China, India, western Asia, and much of Europe, women rarely occupied the throne and almost never held any position of power. Since nearly all surviving documents from the ancient world were written by men and concern their own political and social activities, however, women's contributions may have been overlooked.

▶ In ancient civilizations a woman's work was generally in the home. This Greek terra-cotta figure, dating from around 575 BCE, shows a woman preparing the dough for baking bread.

Women in Politics

In every society there were women who defied the conventions. Although the great majority of Egypt's rulers, for example, were men, there were notable exceptions. During a reign of around fifteen years (c. 1473–1458 BCE), Hatshepsut governed Egypt with considerable success. Other female rulers of Egypt included Sebeknefru (reigned c. 1789–1786 BCE) and Cleopatra (51–30 BCE). Nefertiti was an extremely influential figure during the reign of her husband Akhenaten (1352–1336 BCE). Boudicca became queen of the British Iceni tribe on the death of her husband in 60 CE. In the Roman Empire, many women exerted influence from behind the scenes, as

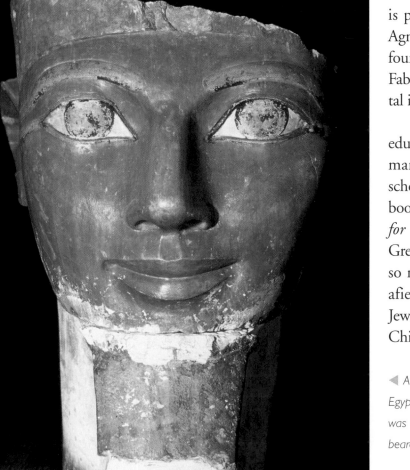

Nefertiti had done. Messalina, as wife of Emperor Claudius (reigned 41–54 CE), and Agrippina the Younger, as niece of Claudius and mother of Nero (reigned 54–68), made a considerable mark on history. *Biographies of Heroic Women*, by Liu Xiang (79–8 BCE), includes several examples of such women in ancient China.

Other Prominent Women

Although women in ancient societies were generally excluded from jobs in medicine, law, and the arts, some managed to rise to positions of influence in these professions. Peseshet was the overseer of female doctors in Egypt aound 2350 BCE; her job title itself is proof that Egypt had female doctors. Agnodice was a Greek gynecologist of the fourth century CE, and the Roman woman Fabiola founded Europe's first public hospital in the fourth century CE.

Despite their exclusion from formal education, a handful of women made their mark as intellectuals. The great Chinese scholar Ban Zhao (c. 45–116 CE) wrote a book on female virtues called *Admonitions for Girls;* Hypatia, the fourth-century-CE Greek philosopher and mathematician, was so renowned that scholars came from far afield to hear her teach. Deborah was a Jewish prophetess; Wei Fu-Jen was perhaps China's greatest calligrapher.

◀ *Although a woman, Hatshepsut, who reigned over Egypt in her own right from about 1473 to 1458 BCE, was known as king and wore the ceremonial royal false beard.*

SEE ALSO

Writing

Writing is a means of communicating in which visible marks represent units of a spoken language. Even the simplest spoken languages are extremely complex systems, combining small units of sound in elaborate ways and governed by sophisticated rules of grammar and syntax. The development of writing required an advanced understanding of how language works. Some early civilizations, notably those in the Americas, never devised effective writing systems.

Writing and Civilization

Writing became a principal driving force of human development. It enabled the present to be recorded for the future. Thus, information and ideas could be handed down from generation to generation, and people were able to build upon what had gone before them. Without writing, the transmission of ideas from one generation to another was a much slower and less reliable process. Indeed, all but the most simple mathematics, philosophy, law, science, and history are unimaginable without writing.

In most areas, writing developed in four stages: picture writing, word-based writing, sound-based writing, and alphabet writing. The last stage, the invention of the alphabet, was one of the greatest of all human achievements.

Sumerian Writing

One of the earliest writing systems was used by the Sumerians, who lived in southern Mesopotamia (present-day southern Iraq). Sumerian writing grew out of the practice of making clay shapes to represent objects. These clay shapes date back as far as 8000 BCE. Some 4,500 years later, around 3500 BCE, people were inscribing clay tablets with marks that represented these shapes. (It is significant that writing—like civilization itself—began in areas where clay was plentiful.) These marks, or symbols, are among the earliest examples of writing. They seem to have been used to record business transactions.

▼ Inscribed on a clay tablet around 2600 BCE, this Sumerian document in wedge-shaped cuneiform writing details the sale of a house and field.

Writing Words

In time the shapes that represented objects became more like symbols than exact pictures of the objects they represented. Symbolic shapes were also used to represent concepts—"hope," for example. In Sumer the stylus used to inscribe on the wet clay left a wedge-shaped indentation. The writing became known as *cuneiform*, from the Latin *cuneus,* meaning "wedge."

By the third millennium BCE, as the Sumerian writing system was taken up by the Akkadians, Assyrians, and Babylonians, it became more sound based. Thus, the symbol for a particular object could represent not only the object itself but also the sound of the word for that object. An equivalent in English would be to use a picture of an eye and a picture of a deer to stand for the word *idea.*

Egypt and China

Egyptian writing, which used symbols known as hieroglyphs, seems to have emerged toward the end of the fourth millennium BCE, a little before Sumerian cuneiform. Archaeological evidence suggests that Egyptian writing developed independently of cuneiform and was invented as a complete system rather than developing from an earlier primitive system. Although many Egyptian hieroglyphs are pictures of objects, the majority represent sounds or combinations of sounds.

Chinese writing (from which Japanese writing derived) was well developed by the Shang dynasty (eighteenth–twelfth century BCE). Each symbol, or character, represented one sound. As there were thousands of single sounds in Chinese, each with a different meaning, learning to write the Chinese language was (and still is) an arduous task.

Clay to Paper

The first writing was either scraped on wet clay or carved on stone or wood. Although it lasted, this form of writing was not very

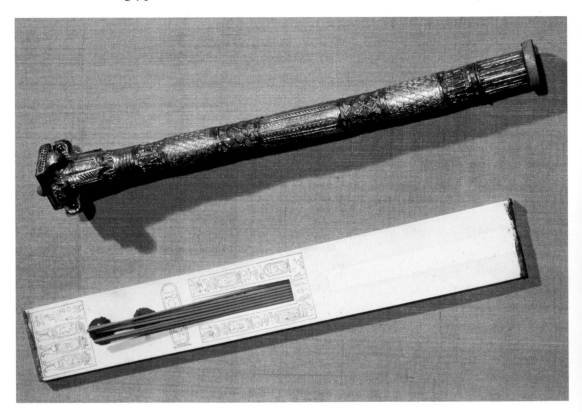

▶ This case for holding writing reeds, pen, and palette were found in the tomb of King Tutankhamen (reigned c. 1336–1327 BCE).

THE ALPHABET

uring the second millennium BCE, somewhere in the region of the eastern Mediterranean, the first alphabet started to take shape. It was based on the principle of breaking down sounds into their smallest units—a p or a t, for example—and devising a symbol for each of these units. By putting different symbols together, any combination of words could be made.

All alphabets seem to have grown out of a single alphabet, used to write down an ancient Semitic language. The final touch was added by the Greeks around 900 BCE. They used the Semitic alphabet for their own language, adding letters for the five vowel sounds. Previous writing systems had left vowels unwritten. The word alphabet comes from alpha and beta, the first two letters of the Greek alphabet.

portable. The solution, discovered in the second millennium BCE, was to write with ink on a light, flexible surface. The Egyptians made an early form of paper from beaten papyrus reeds. Other civilizations wrote on dried animal skins (parchment). About two thousand years ago the Chinese invented true paper, which they made by pulping wood and rags.

The Power of the Word

The invention of writing systems transformed civilization. In government codes of law were set down, in religion sacred texts were recorded, and in science and mathematics theories and principles were written down. Literature and education were born.

The invention of writing gave great power to those who could read and write. In Egypt and China particularly, the scribe was a key figure. Many kings and emperors were not literate, and it was vital to have at court scribes of the utmost skill, reliability and honesty. The ruler's reputation ultimately rested in their hands.

◀ This Egyptian carving, from about 1250 BCE, shows Seshat, the goddess of writing, holding a notched palm rib, which symbolized the passing of time.

SEE ALSO

- Akkadians • Babylonians • China • Egypt • Greece, Classical
- Languages • Literature • Mesopotamia • Mycenaean Civilization
- Prehistory

Xerxes

Xerxes (in old Persian, Khshayarsa), a king of the Achaemenid dynasty, reigned from 519 to 465 BCE. He strengthened his empire by crushing rebellions in the Persian provinces. When his father, Darius I, died in 486, Xerxes inherited both the Persian Empire and his father's aim of defeating the Greek city-states of Athens and Sparta.

Succession

As a younger son of King Darius, Xerxes was not first in line to the throne. However, his mother, Atossa, was the daughter of Cyrus the Great and as such had much influence at the Persian court. Atossa made sure that Xerxes was named heir.

The Invasion of Greece

In 482 BCE Xerxes began to gather together an army and navy that was probably the largest force assembled by any ruler up to that time. The Greek historian Herodotus reported that Xerxes had an army of 1,700,000 men and a fleet of 1,207 triremes, but these figures were almost certainly exaggerated. Nevertheless, it took seven days for the Persian army to cross the wooden bridges that Xerxes had ordered his engineers to build over the Hellespont—the narrow stretch of water that separates Asia Minor (then part of the Persian Empire) from the Greek territories.

At first Xerxes was all conquering. His fleet won a victory at Artemisium, and his army slaughtered the small Spartan army at the Pass of Thermopylae. Xerxes took the deserted city of Athens and set fire to it and in doing so destroyed many of its fine temples. However, his battle fleet was destroyed in the narrow straits of Salamis in September 480, and his army was defeated at Plataea the following year.

▶ According to Herodotus, Xerxes prayed to the gods before he watched his troops march across the Hellespont from Asia into Europe. The Persian army was so large that it took seven days and nights to cross the wooden bridge.

IN 490 BCE THE ATHENIANS AND THEIR PLATAEAN ALLIES DEFEATED DARIUS AT THE BATTLE OF MARATHON. XERXES WAS DETERMINED TO AVENGE HIS FATHER BY CONQUERING GREECE:

I will march an army through Europe into Greece and punish the Athenians for the outrage they committed upon my father.... Darius himself was preparing for war against the Greeks but death prevented him from carrying out his purpose.... I will not rest until I have taken Athens and burned it to the ground in revenge for the injury that the Athenians did to my father.

HERODOTUS, HISTORIES, 7:VIIIA

Iron Fist

Xerxes seems to have been a tougher ruler than other Persian kings of the Achaemenid dynasty (generally dated from the start of Cyrus's reign in 550 to the defeat of Darius III by Alexander the Great in 330). During the early years of his reign, Xerxes put down rebellions in Babylon and Egypt; both lost their special status as kingdoms and became merely satrapies, or districts. The golden statue of Marduk was removed from Babylon, and the two statues of Darius at Heliopolis in Egypt were moved to Xerxes' capital at Susa. Xerxes tried to force his subjects to worship only the Persian god Ahura Mazda, although many scholars believe that this order was not strictly enforced.

Stagnation

After Plataea, Xerxes reigned for another fourteen years, but little is known about this period of his life. Some scholars believe that he was King Ahasuerus, who, according to the Book of Esther in the Old Testament, protected the Jews from persecution. Others believe that Persia suffered decline and stagnation in his later years. Xerxes was murdered in 465, after a plot was hatched by the grand vizier (the king's chief adviser) and his chamberlain (the chief servant of a household).

SEE ALSO

• Achaemenids • Ahura Mazda • Cyrus the Great • Darius I

Zapotecs

The Zapotec people lived in the Oaxaca region of southern Mexico. They settled in the valleys that lie east and west of the modern town of Oaxaca and established one of the first major cities of the region, Monte Albán, in about 500 BCE. Like the Olmec people before them and the Mayan civilization that followed, the Zapotecs had powerful rulers who believed their destiny to command was given to them by the gods.

The oldest town in the region, Teotitlan del Valle, was probably a trading center where the Zapotec (and later the Mixtec) people bought and sold food. The valleys were fertile enough to grow vegetables and fruit, although monuments to the rain god suggest people could not always depend on a water supply. The basic food grown was maize.

▼ *Zapotec and Olmec territory in present-day central Mexico.*

Some cities, including Yagul, were built on high ground so that they had a view of the surrounding area, which provided early warning of any enemy attack. More often, though, the position was a demonstration of power over local inhabitants and those of neighboring regions.

Religion

Religious worship took many forms. Pyramids were built to house the tombs of the dead, whose lives were held in high honor by their descendants. As it was difficult to collect water on hilltops, the rain god was one of the most important deities. Monuments to this god can be found in many cities. At Monte Albán the central plaza was designed to ease the god's task: the floors were on a slight slope so that rainwater could be collected more easily.

Zapotec Carvings

Many Zapotec stone carvings remain and suggest a civilization whose history was marked by violence and a strong emphasis on ceremony and ritual. At Monte Albán there are several monuments to enemies killed in battle, as well as carvings of captives who were killed in violent rituals—a display of power to would-be rivals.

At Dainzu there is an ancient ball court, as well as carved stone reliefs showing ball-court players. At Mitla the palace walls are

decorated with geometric mosaics made up of thousands of square- and diamond-shaped stones. There are fifteen patterns, many in rectangular boxes, that seem to symbolize natural elements such as clouds, rain, and lightning. Other patterns have been shown to resemble the skin of the *crotalus*, a local rattlesnake with intricate diamond-shaped patterns on its back. The Zapotecs also made carvings out of jade, a dark green stone. One of the most striking examples of Zapotec carving is a bat-god pendant with staring eyes, believed to be a messenger of death.

ZAPOTECS

500 BCE

Zapotec cities are established at Yagul and Monte Albán.

200 BCE to 200 CE

Monte Albán flourishes as the center of Zapotec rule.

800 CE

Monte Albán declines and Zapotec influence wanes.

◀ *The corner of the courtyard in the main temple at Mitla.*

ZAPOTEC WRITING

Although archaeologists have uncovered many examples of Zapotec writing, experts are still a long way from being able to read the hieroglyphs of the Zapotecs in the same way that Egyptian and Mayan hieroglyphs can be read. Some scholars believe that place-names are symbolized by landmarks, that verbs of actions are symbolized in hand shapes, and that other glyphs relate information about politics and religious ritual. There is some evidence that the Zapotec system of writing developed into the later writing systems of the Mayan, Mixtec, and Aztec civilizations.

▲ The ball court at Monte Albán.

Recording Time and History

The Zapotecs were one of the first civilizations to measure the passing of time and the seasons. The calendar of the 260-day year used by the Maya came from Zapotec observations. The Zapotecs observed that twice a year the sun reached its zenith and shone directly overhead: in other words, objects in the open cast no shadow.

At Monte Albán, there is a narrow vertical shaft in the temple known as Building P. At the two zeniths, in May and August, the sun shines straight down this shaft and illuminates a stone slab at the bottom. These times of year may have been important to the Zapotecs for reasons of climate change or cultivation. Alternatively, they may have been good times to give displays of power or control over neighbors and rivals. The two zeniths in the calendar are recorded in other places in the form of a double-headed serpent.

Zapotec Stelae

The Zapotecs were among the first peoples to record important moments in time by means of glyphs. Glyphs, carvings in stone that took the form of pictures and symbols, were often placed on vertical columns known as stelae, which marked the passage of time and also served as a record of battles, victories, and the sacrifice of captives. The stelae often showed the names of rulers and their descendants, their birth, marriage, and death.

Traders or Warriors?

Many miles to the northwest of Oaxaca lies the great city of Teotihuacán. Archaeological evidence at Teotihuacán proves that Zapotec traders visited the city and set up commercial links between the two civilizations. Some experts believe that the decline of Monte Albán was caused by rivalry with its more powerful neighbor.

SEE ALSO

- Maya
- Monte Albán
- Olmecs
- Religion

Zenobia

Zenobia was the wife of Odaenathus, the ruler of Palmyra—a city in present-day Syria that was then part of the Roman Empire—during the third century CE. When Odaenathus was assassinated in 267 CE, his son Wahballet was too young to rule, and so Zenobia acted as regent, ruling on Wahballet's behalf. Well educated and determined, Zenobia was not content to be a puppet of Rome, and she strove to make Palmyra a powerful independent city.

Palmyra was in existence as early as 1800 BCE, and by Roman times it was an important city on a principal trade route that connected Mesopotamia (present-day Iraq) with the Roman world. As governor of Palmyra, Odaenathus remained loyal to the Roman Empire.

Upon her succession, Zenobia named herself queen of Palmyra and gave Wahballet his father's title, Governor of All the East. In 269 CE, only two years after the death of her husband, Zenobia sent an army to attack Egypt as well as a large part of Asia Minor (present-day Turkey). Her declaration of the independence of Palmyra from Roman rule brought retaliation from Rome, and in 271 Zenobia's army was driven out of Egypt. In the following year, the Romans expelled her troops from Asia Minor and later defeated her army at a battle at Emesa, in present-day Syria. Emperor Aurelian, the Roman military leader, then marched his army across 120 miles of desert and laid siege to Palmyra. Zenobia and her son were taken prisoner and brought to Rome. Sometime afterward Zenobia married a Roman senator and lived peacefully at his villa in Italy.

◀ This coin, minted around 274 CE at Alexandria in Egypt, bears the image of Zenobia.

ODAENATHUS *DIED 267 CE*

Zenobia's husband, Odaenathus, was the ruler of Palmyra at a time when Persia was threatening to challenge the Roman Empire in the east. Odaenathus remained loyal to Rome when Persians kidnapped the Roman emperor Valerian and he defeated the army of the Persian king Shapur I in 260 CE. He also fought for Valerian against a rebellious Roman leader who wanted to become emperor. He was rewarded by the son of Valerian with the title Governor of All the East and was allowed to call himself the king of Palmyra. Odaenathus continued to work for Rome by driving the Persians out of Mesopotamia. His success contributed to the restoration of Roman rule in the east. It is possible that the assassination of Odaenathus and his eldest son was carried out on the orders of Zenobia.

In 273 Palmyra rebelled against Rome once more, and Zenobia's family was involved in the uprising. The Romans attacked and defeated the city once again and brought two more sons of Zenobia's to Rome as prisoners. To ensure that Palmyra never again threatened Rome, the city was razed to the ground. The ruins lay undiscovered for centuries and were not found again until the eighteenth century.

Zenobia was by all accounts a remarkable woman. She was well educated and known for her determination, but she was also experienced in politics and managed to survive the unsuccessful challenge that she mounted against Roman rule. Zenobia was also renowned as a wrestler, although this story may well be only a legend.

◀ *This stone sculpture shows Zenobia (seated, left) with a female companion standing beside her.*

SEE ALSO

• Mesopotamia
• Roman Republic and Empire • Sasanians

Zeus

Zeus was the king of the Olympian gods of ancient Greece. His weapon, the thunderbolt, suggests that he evolved from an earlier sky god. It is not known exactly when Zeus was first worshiped, but temples to Zeus are named on Mycenean stone tablets from the thirteenth century BCE. As Greece was absorbed into the Roman Empire—a gradual process completed around 150 BCE—the Romans adopted Greek mythology and identified Zeus with their chief god, Jupiter.

Zeus was the youngest son of Rhea and Cronus. Cronus swallowed all his children except Zeus, whom Rhea managed to save. When Zeus grew up, he rescued his brothers and sisters and led them against Cronus and the other old gods (the Titans). Zeus and the Olympian gods defeated the Titans and cast them down into Tartarus, part of the underworld, where they suffered eternal punishment.

This myth suggests that, at some point in Greek history, Zeus replaced Cronus as the king of the gods. This change may have happened when invaders replaced an existing culture with their own.

Although Zeus was supreme ruler of the universe, he was aided by his brothers Poseidon (who became the Roman god Neptune) and Hades (Pluto). Zeus married Metis, Themis, and finally, his sister Hera (Juno), who is his queen in most Greek myths. Zeus fathered other gods by his three wives but also many demigods by mortal women. One of the most famous demigods was Herakles (Hercules).

Zeus often angered Hera by pursuing beautiful nymphs and human women. He seduced them by changing his shape into something apparently harmless. To overpower Leda, he became a swan, and for Europa he was a white bull.

▼ Cronus, warned that a son of his would one day overthrow him, swallowed all his children except Zeus, who escaped when Rhea tricked her husband by giving him a stone wrapped in napkins.

Zeus found his way to Danae, imprisoned by her father, by turning himself into a shower of gold. Such disguises were not only a trick but also served to protect the women from the terrible power of Zeus's divine appearance.

Zeus, who was immensely strong, was seen as a god of justice and wisdom who punished wrongdoers. For example, when Prometheus stole fire for mankind, Zeus had him chained to a rock in the Caucasus Mountains with a vulture forever tearing out his liver.

Worship of Zeus

Zeus was worshiped with burned offerings of meat, and with games. His oracle at Dodona was said to be the oldest in Greece. He also had a magnificent temple at Olympia, where his gold and ivory statue was one of the Seven Wonders of the Ancient World. The ruins of Zeus's temple in Athens still stand.

Worship of Zeus continued into the fourth century CE. The Christian Roman emperor Constantine began to restrict pagan religion in 324 CE, but Emperor Theodosius still found it necessary to ban worship of Zeus in 393 CE.

▶ *A first-century-CE Roman marble of Zeus, king of the Olympian gods.*

HESIOD, WRITING AROUND 700 BCE, DESCRIBES THE JUSTICE OF ZEUS:

For those who practice violent and cruel deeds far-seeing Zeus, son of Cronus, ordains a punishment. Often a whole city suffers for the sins of one bad man who presumes to offend the gods. The son of Cronus inflicts disaster upon the people: famine and plague together. The men perish, the women bear no children, and their houses become few, all through the will of Olympian Zeus. At another time, the son of Cronus destroys their great army or their walls, or wrecks their ships on the sea.

HESIOD, WORKS AND DAYS

SEE ALSO
• Greek Mythology
• Religion
• Roman Mythology

Zoroastrianism

Zoroastrianism, the religion of the ancient Persians, is often described as the first world religion. It originated in the ideas and teachings of the Iranian prophet Zarathustra (called Zoroaster by the Greeks), who condemned the old sacrifice cults of the Persians. For over a thousand years Zoroastrianism was a very important religion and still has many adherents. Zoroastrian ideas spread far beyond Persia and influenced Buddhist, Greek, and early Christian thinkers.

Zoroastrianism had a strong influence on the religious practices of the Achaemenid kings, whose period of rule is traditionally dated from 550 to 330 BCE. Under the Sasanian kings, who ruled from 224 to 636 CE, Zoroastrianism became the official state religion of Persia. This state of affairs ended in the seventh century with the arrival of Islam. When they were persecuted by the new Muslim rulers of Iran, many Zoroastrians fled to India, where Zoroastrianism survived among the Parsee community.

Zarathustra's Beliefs

Early Persians believed in demons and worshiped many gods. Zarathustra believed they should worship only one god, the god of light and goodness, whom he called the Wise Lord Ahura Mazda. Zarathustra believed that Ahura Mazda was locked in a cosmic struggle with Ahriman, the leader of the evil spirits. Ordinary men and women had a role to play in the spiritual battle between good and evil. By living a good life, they helped Ahura Mazda and strengthened the forces of goodness.

◀ Like many Persian religious artists, the sixth-century-BCE sculptor of these winged sphinxes from the Persian royal palace at Susa, shown under the emblem of Ahura Mazda, borrowed from motifs used in earlier Assyrian and Egyptian art.

Zarathustra also believed that history was divided into three ages. In the first age, the world had been perfect and ruled by goodness. In the second (present) age, evil was at large. Zarathustra believed that perfect goodness would return to the world and that ordinary people could hasten this golden age by leading good lives.

Zarathustra's teachings also included practical advice on agriculture and animal rearing. He believed that the ability to look after the earth and care for its plants and animals was one sign of a good and wise man. Many centuries after his death, Zarathustra's ideas were written down in the holy scriptures of Zoroastrianism. These are the sacred books known as the Zend Avesta.

Zoroastrian Customs

Persian children took part in Zoroastrian ceremonies from the age of seven onward. A believer prayed and performed a complicated cleansing ritual five times each day. At especially holy times of the year, Zoroastrians drank a sacred liquid called *haoma*. This drink was made by straining a special herb and fermenting it until it turned into an alcolohic liquor. After drinking *haoma*, the Magi (high priests) chanted spells to cast out evil demons.

Fire also played a big part in Zoroastrian rituals. Fire represented the light of the sky and the power of the sun. The Persian kings and their Magi worshiped at special fire altars near their palaces at Pasargadae and Persepolis. Unlike

▼ *Modern Parsees still follow the ancient rituals of their faith. This young Parsee boy receives a knotted belt of lamb's wool, a symbol of purity, from his priest.*

▶ Naqsh-e Rustam, near Persepolis, was a very holy place for the Persian kings, many of whom are buried there. These Zoroastrian fire altars date from the time of the Sasanian kings (224–636 CE).

Christians and Jews, Zoroastrians were allowed to marry their close relatives. Persian nobles even married their sisters and nieces to stop their blood from being mixed with that of commoners. Zoroastrians believed that the soul survived after death. The soul of a believer who had lived a good life entered a realm of brilliant light where Ahura Mazda reigned.

Zoroastrian Funeral Practices

Zoroastrians believed that it was wrong to contaminate, or pollute, the pure and holy elements of fire and water. They could not therefore bury or cremate their dead. Instead, a corpse was placed on a stone platform, sometimes called the Tower of Silence, and left there for weeks until the flesh had been stripped from the skeleton by vultures or other birds of prey. The bones were then taken and stored in an *astodan*, or ossuary. Only special slaves called *nassesalars*, or corpse bearers, could touch the dead or their bones.

ZARATHUSTRA

Very little is known for certain about the founder of Zoroastrianism. Zarathustra was probably born in northwestern Iran. His name may mean "one who handles camels." According to tradition, he belonged to the Spitama clan, and as a young man, he worked as a priest whose duty it was to prepare and offer sacrifices. At the age of thirty, he had a series of divine visions after spending seven years meditating in a desert cavern. He believed that he had been given a holy message by the supreme god, Ahura Mazda. Failing to win converts to his ideas in his homeland, he fled to Khorasmia in eastern Iran, where he converted King Vishtaspa, who may have been Hystaspes, the father of Darius. Thanks to this royal influence, Zoroastrian ideas spread throughout the Persian kingdom.

It is not known when Zarathustra lived. Zoroastrians believe that he was born between 630 and 618 BCE. Most modern scholars think that he was born much earlier. The style of the earliest Zoroastrian writings suggests that he probably lived and worked between around 1000 and 930 BCE. Unfortunately, it is not certain how much of the early Zoroastrian scriptures was written by the prophet himself and how much by his later followers.

▲ *The Tower of Silence at Yazd in present-day Iran.*

At first only the corpses of the Magi, or Persian high priests, were exposed in this way. Other important Persians, such as the Achaemenid kings, were covered in a thick layer of wax when they died and then placed in tightly sealed stone chambers. These chambers were placed in caves cut high into the rock of the sheer cliffs at Naqsh-e Rustam, near Persepolis. They were buried with great care to make sure that no part of the royal corpse leaked into the environment.

THE MAGI

The Magi were originally a priestly tribe that came from Medea in western Iran. They were ateshperest, or fire worshipers, and kept alive the ancient gods and rituals of the Aryan peoples. By 500 BCE, however, many of them had become followers of Zarathustra and worshiped Ahura Mazda. In Achaemenid times, important Magi acted as high priests to the king. They interpreted his dreams and gave him advice on the sacred rituals that he had to perform.

The Magi were often learned men who studied ancient languages and the sciences, especially astronomy. Under the Sasanian kings, the Magi became the official priesthood of the state. By 500 CE, some of the Magi had become very wealthy and corrupt and had lost touch with the ordinary people. Their growing unpopularity may be one of the reasons why many Persians abandoned Zoroastrianism and converted to Islam in the seventh century.

SEE ALSO
- Achaemenids
- Ahura Mazda
- Aryans
- Death and Burial
- Sasanians

Glossary

alluvial Describing the environment, action, and sedimentary deposits of rivers or streams.

antler pick A digging tool made from the hard, bony antlers of deer. It was used like a pick, to loosen soil and force rock and stone from the ground.

basilica A large oblong building with two rows of columns and an apse (a domed semicircular section).

bluestone A type of hard stone that is bluish gray in dry weather.

caravan A column of merchants traveling, usually on camels, across desert country.

cenotaph A monument to a person who is buried elsewhere.

fuchsite A hard dark green rock used in carvings.

hippodrome An open air stadium in ancient Greece or Rome with an oval track that was used for horse or chariot racing.

keel The V-shaped bottom of a ship.

lacquer To finish wooden bowls and other containers by painting them with lacquer, liquid sap from the lacquer tree. The artist applies several coats of lacquer, which then dry to form a tough, glossy finish.

lapis lazuli A bright blue mineral used as a gemstone.

lintel A timber beam or stone block placed across the top of a pair of standing stones.

matriarchal Describing a society or family in which the governing authority is held by women.

maul stone A heavy stone used as a hammer.

monolith A single large block of stone.

nave The main central part of a church.

necropolis Literally, "city of the dead": a place where a great many dead people are buried and where temples and chapels are dedicated to them.

nymph A minor goddess or spirit of nature in mythology; a nymph inhabited areas of natural beauty, such as woods, mountains, and rivers, and was traditionally regarded as a beautiful young woman.

obsidian A type of hard, sharp volcanic glass used by many ancient civilizations to make spear tips and cutting tools.

oracle A shrine where ancient Greeks consulted a god for advice or a prophecy; also, the priestess through whom the god was thought to speak.

ossuary A chamber for storing human bones.

Parsee Member of a Zoroastrian community in India that left Persia in the seventh and eighth centuries.

patriarchal Describing a society or family in which the governing authority is held by men.

sarcophagus A stone container used to hold the body of a dead person.

sarsen A type of hard sandstone. In Britain sarsen was used for the construction of prehistoric monuments such as Avebury and Stonehenge.

scepter A ceremonial rod carried as a symbol of power.

shadoof A water-raising device used in ancient Egypt and India consisting of a suspended pivoting pole with a bucket on one end and a counterweight on the other.

shroud The cloth in which a dead person is wrapped.

siren In Greek legend, a beautiful woman who by singing sweetly lured sailors onto the rocks.

syntax The rules governing the way in which words may be arranged and combined.

tributary A river or stream that flows into a larger one or into a lake.

tribute Payment made by one state or tribe to another as a sign of submission.

trilithon Two upright stones supporting a third to form a kind of arch or doorway; from the Greek for "three stones."

trireme A ship powered by oarsmen on three levels.

Index

Page numbers in **boldface type** refer to main articles.
Page numbers in *italic type* refer to illustrations.